Homeschooling in Oregon:

The Handbook

Ann Lahrson

Homeschooling in Oregon: The Handbook
By Ann Lahrson

Published by
OUT OF THE BOX PUBLISHING
PO Box 80214-B
Portland, Oregon 97280
(503)244-9677

First printing, 1994.
Second printing, 1995.
Printed in the United States of America

Cover design by Katharine Sammons, Panic Graphic Design.

(503) 222-6840

ISBN 0-9640813-7-7

Lahrson, Ann
    Homeschooling In Oregon: The Handbook / Ann Lahrson

    Included index and bibliographical references.
    ISBN 0-9640813-7-7
    1. Homeschooling — United States. 2. Homeschooling — Oregon.
        3. Homeschooling — Resources. 4. Education —
        Home-based. I. Title.
    LC40
    649.68
    CIP Library of Congress Catalog Card Number 94-65549

FOR ALICE AND ERIN

who still turn my life upside down,
for which I am nearly always grateful.

What we want is to see
the child in pursuit of knowledge,
and not
knowledge in pursuit of the child.
— George Bernard Shaw

TABLE OF CONTENTS

PART ONE
BASIC INFORMATION

PART TWO
HOW-TO-HOMESCHOOL
RESOURCES

PART THREE
CURRICULUM RESOURCES

PART FOUR
RELIGIOUS RESOURCES

APPENDIXES

I have never let my schooling interfere
with my education.
-Mark Twain

FOREWORD

Nurturing Children's Natural Love Of Learning

As homeschooling parents, my husband and I sometimes wonder who is learning more in our family, the parents or the children. The topic we seem to be learning most about is the nature of learning itself. The term "homeschooling," however, has proven to be misleading: These children do not spend all of their time at home, nor is their learning approached in the same way that it would be in school. In fact, many of the assumptions about learning found in public school teaching are reversed in homeschooling.

The main element in successful homeschooling is trust. We trust the children to know when they are ready to learn and what they are interested in learning. We trust them to know how to go about learning. While this may seem to be an astonishing way of looking at children, parents commonly take this view of learning during the child's first two years, when he is learning to stand, walk, talk and to perform many other important and difficult things, without any help from anyone.

No one worries that a baby will be too lazy, uncooperative or unmotivated to learn these things; it is simply assumed that every baby is born wanting to learn the things he needs to know in order to understand and to participate in the world around him. These one- and two-year old experts teach us several principles of learning:

Children are naturally curious and have a built-in desire to learn about the world around them. John Holt, in *How Children Learn*, describes the natural learning style of young children:

The child is curious. He wants to make sense out of things, find out how things work, gain competence and control over himself and his environment, and do what he can see other people doing. He is open, perceptive and experimental. He does not merely observe the world around him, but tastes it, touches it, hefts it, bends it, breaks it. To find out how reality works, he works on it. He is bold. And he is patient. He can tolerate an extraordinary amount of uncertainty, confusion, ignorance and suspense...School is not a place that gives much time, or opportunity, or reward, for this kind of thinking and learning.

Children know best how to go about learning something. If left alone, they will know instinctively what method is best for them. Parents say to their baby, "Oh, that's interesting! You're learning how to crawl downstairs by facing backwards!" They do not say, "That's the wrong way." Perceptive parents are aware that there are many different ways to learn something, and they trust their children to know which ways are best for them.

Children need large amounts of quiet time to think. Research shows that children who are good at fantasizing are better learners and cope better with disappointment. But fantasy requires time, and time is the most endangered commodity in our lives. Fully scheduled school hours and extra-curricular activities leave little time for children to dream, to think, to invent solutions to problems, to cope with bad experiences, and simply to fulfill the universal need for solitude and privacy.

Children are not afraid to admit ignorance and to make mistakes. When Holt invited toddlers to play his cello, they would eagerly attempt to do so; schoolchildren and adults would invariably decline.

Homeschooling children, free from the threats of public embarrassment and failing marks, retain their openness to new explorations. Children learn by asking questions, not by answering them. Toddlers ask many questions, and so do schoolchildren — until about grade three; by that time many of them have learned to hide ignorance.

Children take joy in the intrinsic values of whatever they are learning. There is no need to motivate children through the use of extrinsic rewards, which suggest to the child that the activity must be difficult or unpleasant. The wise parent says, "You're really enjoying that picture book!", not "If you look at this book you'll get a cookie!"

Children learn best about getting along with other people through interaction with those of all ages. No parents would tell their baby, "You can only spend time with children whose birthdays are within six months of your own. Here's another two-year-old to play with. You can look at each other, but no talking!" John Taylor Gatto, New York City's Teacher of the Year, contends, "It is absurd, and anti-life to...sit in confinement with people of exactly the same age and social class. That system effectively cuts you off from the immense diversity of life."

A child learns best about the world through first-hand experience. No parent would tell her toddler, "Let's put that caterpillar down and get back to your book about caterpillars." Homeschoolers learn directly about the world. Our son describes homeschooling as "learning by doing instead of being taught." Ironically, the most common objection to homeschooling is that the children are "being deprived of the real world!"

Children need and deserve ample time with their family. Gatto warns us, "Between schooling and television, all the time children have is eaten up. That's what has destroyed the American family." Many homeschoolers feel that family cohesiveness is perhaps the most meaningful benefit of the experience. Just as I saw his first step and heard his first word, I have the honor and privilege of sharing my son's world and thoughts. I have learned much from him about life and love and what's truly important.

Stress interferes with learning. Einstein wrote, "It is a very grave mistake to think that the enjoyment of seeing and searching can be promoted by means of correction." When a one-year-old falls down while learning to walk, we say, "Good try! You'll catch on soon!" No caring parent would say, "Every baby your age should be walking . . . you'd better be walking by Friday!"

Most parents understand how difficult it is for their children to learn something when they are failing or rushed or threatened. John Holt warns, "We think badly, and even perceive badly, or not at all, when we are anxious or afraid...when we make children afraid, we stop learning dead in its tracks."

While infants and toddlers teach us many principles about learning, schools have adopted quite different principles, due to the difficulties inherent in teaching a large number of same-age children in a compulsory setting. The structure of school (required attendance, school-selected topics and books, and constant checking of the child's progress) implies that children are not naturally learners, but must be compelled to learn through the efforts of others.

Natural learners do not need such a structure. The success of self-directed learning (homeschoolers regularly outperform their schooled peers on measures of academic achievement, socialization, confidence and self-esteem) suggests that structured approaches inhibit both learning and personal development.

Homeschooling is one attempt to follow the principles of natural learning and to help children retain the curiosity, enthusiasm and love of learning which every child has from birth.

Homeschooling, as John Holt writes, is a matter of faith. This faith is that by nature people are learning animals. Birds fly; fish swim; humans think and learn. Therefore, we do not need to motivate children into learning by wheedling, bribing or bullying. We do not need to keep picking away at their minds to make sure they are learning. What we need to do — and all we need to do — is to give children as much help and guidance as they need and ask for, listen respectfully when they feel like talking, and then get out of the way. We can trust them to do the rest.

—JAN HUNT

Jan Hunt is a homeschooling parent, writer, and children's advocate. A former resident of Bend, Oregon, she now resides in Canada.

INTRODUCTION

Using The Handbook

More than ever before, parents have reason to be concerned about their children's education. Many now consider homeschooling their children to be a choice that is as reasonable as public, private, or parochial schooling.

Homeschooling in Oregon is designed to help you make intelligent choices about your child's education. It will reassure you, as parents, that yes, if you want to, you can homeschool your children.

You will find information about getting started, networking, state requirements, curriculum planning, national and local resources, testing, apprenticeships, college, and more.

This book that began as a notebook listing a few popular materials has literally exploded into the book you have in your hands. The resources available to homeschoolers are growing at such a rapid rate that it would not be possible to list all the materials that are available. A selection of the most useful and recognized services and materials that are currently available are included.

To help you find the kind of help you need, I have divided the book into four parts.

Part One is **Basic Information,** important for people who are new to homeschooling, and will help you get a sense of what homeschooling is like. It includes a potpourri of selected topics of interest to the Oregon homeschooling parent. These discussions do not provide a complete discussion of homeschooling issues, but they are a good place to begin.

Part Two is the **How-To Section.** In Part Two you can find a person, group, book, or magazine that can provide you with in depth discussions on many homeschooling issues, including a few issues that may surprise you. In other words, you can probably find at least one, if not several, resources that will help you solve even the most obscure question about homeschooling. You are probably only a phone call or two away from the information that you need.

Part Three is the **Curriculum Resources—the Learner's Tool Kit**, and includes curriculum materials, programs, services, resources, and ideas: what the children — and you — do all day long. Traditional materials and resources are listed, along with many educational resources that are unique. Be sure to look through the children's periodicals, local community resources, and other sections that might give you some new ideas about ways that children can learn.

Part Four includes **Religious Resources** that are used by homeschoolers from three faiths: Christianity, Judaism, and Islam.

Need I mention that this book is a work in progress? Addresses and phone numbers change, and companies come and go, almost as fast as I type. I apologize for any wild goose chases you encounter in your attempts to find resources.

Errors and oversights are inevitable. I have been hard-pressed to keep up with new information as it comes in. You may be aware of excellent materials that are not included. Letters from readers who find errors, or who have suggestions, corrections, or updated information, will be gratefully appreciated, and will be noted for a possible future edition.

Some materials that I have found particularly useful, informative, or enjoyable are marked with **R**. Other materials are listed without judgment. Some materials have been suggested by other homeschooling parents. I have not reviewed all of the materials listed, nor have I read all the books on the book lists.

A Note on Homeschooling Styles

You may notice that much of the material in the handbook focuses on a relaxed style of homeschooling, rather than a traditional model of how to "do school" at home. There are several reasons for this emphasis:

First, traditional schools permit only a few minutes a day of one-on-one contact between student and teacher, while the essence of homeschooling is one-on-one contact. One-on-one instruction is a highly efficient educational method for the learner. Learning happens fast when a child is both ready and interested in a subject.

Years of experience teaching in classrooms, teaching my children at home, and observing other homeschooling families have taught me that traditional instructional methods are designed for large groups of children. Different models of instruction are necessary in order to fully take advantage of the opportunity of homeschooling.

Second, parents who wish to provide a traditional type "school at home" already have a model of such a school in their minds. They can draw from their personal schooling experiences and repeat the good experiences with their own children. In addition, there are many other books and resources available to help you provide a conventionally structured homeschool if that is what you want. (Some of the more structured references are listed in Chapter 11, and others are listed in Chapter 27.)

Finally, the material in this book reflects "state of the art" knowledge of how people learn. Children's minds are not little buckets to be filled with facts. Rather, their minds have a wondrous capacity to think and learn, grow and analyze, and to construct knowledge through their own experiences. This capacity should be respected as we, their parents and teachers, help them to discover their world.

For more discussion about homeschooling styles, and how to find your own style, read Chapter 4.

If you are new to homeschooling, this handbook should help you strike a balance as you develop your family's homeschooling lifestyle. If you already know the ropes, you will find some new resources to try. I hope you will be as happy as I am to have all these resources under one cover. Enjoy!

Emergency Kit!

Help!!!! I just pulled my kids out of school, and bought this book on my way home! I don't know where to start!

This homeschool emergency kit may help:

- First, relax! A day without doing math problems is not necessarily a day wasted. Some families take a family trip when they begin to homeschool. Others just spend time together as a family while they decide what course their homeschool will take. Give the kids get a chance to explore their interests while parents learn about homeschooling.

- Read, read, read. If you read this book, some of the books listed in Chapter 11, and subscribe to a magazine or two from Chapter 10, you will be well on your way to discovering the best way for you to homeschool. If you have special concerns (TAG, LD, ADD, other special needs), learn what you can about others who have dealt with similar issues.

- Listen. Chapter 12 will help you get in touch with local homeschoolers, and homeschoolers throughout the country. Go to support group meetings, events, field trips, conferences and workshops. Get in touch with other homeschooling families. Find out what they do and what they like, and what mistakes they think you should avoid.

- Plan. What will your family study, and how will you go about it? Will you be highly structured, unschooled, or somewhere in between? Consider your homeschooling style, your children's learning styles and interests before you purchase materials. Part Three is a good place to begin.

- Call your local ESD (see Appendix B) and ask for their homeschooling packet. Take the necessary steps to comply with the law (Chapter 2, Appendixes A, B, C, and D).

- Make friends in the homeschooling community. The most successful homeschoolers avoid becoming isolated and get involved with other homeschoolers right away.

- Evaluate your daily routine regularly, at least every month or two until you get the hang of homeschooling. Adapt your plans and goals as necessary.

❖   ❖   ❖

Part One

Basic Information

Freedom is not worth having
if it does not connote freedom to err.
—MAHATMA GANDHI

CHAPTER 1

Questions And Answers About Homeschooling

These questions are frequently asked. If your questions are not answered in this section or elsewhere in the book, you will surely find the answers you seek in one or more of homeschooling reference books listed in Chapter 11, in national magazines listed in Chapter 10, or from a personal contact—see Chapter 12.

Q. What do I have to do to in order to homeschool my children?

A. Homeschooling is legal in Oregon, as well as in all other states. This handbook contains a copy of Oregon's homeschooling law and regulations(Appendix A), an interpretation of the law, and information about how to comply with the law (Chapter 2). Please note: The homeschooling law and regulations are subject to change. For more information, contact the Department of Education or your attorney. To keep up on current homeschooling issues in Oregon, subscribe to a statewide homeschooling newsletter, or join a statewide homeschooling organization.

Q. How do you homeschool?

A. There are as many ways to homeschool as there are people doing it. There are three main options: (1) holding school in your house with structured, regular lessons, perhaps using correspondence schools or prepared structured curriculum; (2) living life and learning through the natural learning process — often called unschooling; or (3) something between the two, which might include cooperative learning, unit studies, individualized curriculums, apprenticeships or work, service activities, student selected curriculum, and more.

Q. What is the difference between homeschooling and unschooling or natural learning?

A. Homeschooling is an inclusive general term that applies to all children between the ages of seven and eighteen who do not attend either public or private school, and who are being educated by a parent or private teacher. It includes all methods of instruction, including strict, curriculum based "school-at-home" at one end of the spectrum and "unschooling" at the other end of the spectrum. Most homeschools fall between the two extremes.

Unschooling describes a method of instruction based on following the child's natural interests. Children who have never been in school may be more accurately described as natural learners. Children are completely removed from the influence of school. They learn naturally, and, if left to discover their own interests along with parental support and guidance, they learn what they need to know.

Q. Isn't homeschooling just for Christians who disagree with what is taught in public schools?

A. Not at all. It is the right of every Oregonian parent to homeschool his or her children, regardless of reasons, faith, or educational philosophy. While many homeschoolers are indeed Christians, many are not. Members of many faiths can be found in the homeschooling community.

Some homeschooling groups and resources focus on meeting the needs of fundamentalist Christian families. Some groups and resources focus on other special interest groups. Still other groups and resources address the general needs of families of all faiths, interests, and educational philosophies. It is important to keep looking until you find resources and support that fit your particular situation.

Q. I am not a trained teacher. How can I be sure that my child is getting the basic education he needs?

A. Let's bury the myth that only certified teachers can teach. Certified teachers are educated in subject matter and the specific large group skills of managing behavior and managing instruction of large groups of children. Homeschooling parents need neither special knowledge in specific subject areas, nor special knowledge in large group instruction and management.

Ask yourself these questions: "Do I enjoy spending time with my children? Do I enjoy learning new things? Am I willing to adapt my lifestyle if needed?" When you teach your own children, you need to enjoy your children and to be willing to spend time with them as they learn. You need to be interested in learning with them, and willing to help them find answers to their questions.

If you are willing to spend your time and energy working with your children, the battle is half won! Your child has the decided advantage of having a private tutor who knows him well, who has her best interests at heart, and who is willing to spend as much time as is needed to help him or her learn. Rarely can a trained teacher offer more than you can if you are willing to do the work!

If you are unsure of your ability to select curriculum, some pre-packaged curricular materials might lend confidence. *The World Book Curriculum Guide* (Chapter 11) is a very inexpensive way to reassure yourself that you are covering the basics. Purchase some textbooks to give you a starting place. Or you can participate in homeschooling programs or correspondence schools mentioned in Part Three.

Q. I wasn't very good in math (or history, or spelling, or French, or whatever) in school. How can I teach my child effectively?

A. First, answer this question for yourself. "Am I willing to learn with my child?"

If you honestly answer "yes," you and your child will do great as you learn together. You will both have a terrific study partner. Get yourself an interesting book on the subject and go for it! Many mothers who hated math as children begin to learn to enjoy it as they work alongside their children. Those childhood math wounds begin to heal, as the mothers begin to realize that they are not stupid after all. A great, hidden pleasure of teaching your own children is discovering for yourself how to learn again.

If, however, you are NOT willing to learn a subject with your child, you can still successfully homeschool. Find another person to work with your child — Dad, Grandma, neighbor, babysitter. You may find another homeschooling family with whom you can trade talents, and homeschool cooperatively. You could trade sewing lessons for math lessons, for example. If finances permit, you might hire a private teacher for that one subject. Some schools may be willing to work with you. Keep looking until you find a satisfactory arrangement.

Q. How am I going to teach my child algebra or physics and other subjects I never learned or feel unqualified to teach?

A. First, if you didn't learn it, you might ponder the question, "Is the subject really all that important to know?" If your answer is, yes, it is important, there are several options: You could learn the subject with your child, or have your spouse work with him. Let your child draw on years of self-schooling and teach himself. Let him work with another homeschooled student. Find a tutor, either a professional in the field, a professional tutor, a college student, another homeschool parent, a teacher, a grandparent or a friend. Contact your local community college for possible classes. See what adult education classes are being (or could be) offered through community centers or schools. Hire a teacher for a group of students. Or if you're in the Portland area, you might try OMSI or Saturday Academy.

Q. What does a typical homeschooling day look like?

A. First, there is no such thing as a typical homeschooling day. Everyone needs to work out what works best for his or her family. Developing your homeschooling style is a gradual process (Chapter 4). After a year of homeschooling, you will begin to set your rhythm and pattern, and this will continue to evolve as your children (and you) grow and change.

People who work with a curriculum or homeschool using traditional school methods often organize their days similar to a school day, with academic lessons in the morning and extra-curricular activities in the afternoon.

Families often relax toward natural learning eventually: answering questions, exploring, taking trips, following subjects of interest, doing chores, taking classes such as gymnastics or piano, participating in clubs such as 4-H or scouts, learning the lessons of life mom and dad think are important, and playing. It is too unnatural to do anything else. Some excellent books about how other families have structured their homeschooling days are mentioned in Chapter 11.

Q. What if my children do nothing but play all day?

A. Your children may indeed spend much of the day playing. This "play" looks different for all children. It may be building tree forts, fantasy play with secret pals, playing house with dolls, making mud pies, tracking animals, working on the computer, creating a play, writing a story, drawing pictures, creating inventions, etc.

Play is whatever a child does. It is how children learn and grow. Play is the way they practice all the emotional, physical, and cognitive skills they will need later in life. It is not easy or trivial. It is vital work. *It is serious and necessary business.*

Play is an expression of creativity, and creativity is a key element in the ability to learn, to cope, and to develop into healthy, contributing individuals. Mathematicians play with numbers and formulas; scientists play with hypotheses and experiments; artists play with color and form; sculptors play with clay; writers play with words; farmers play with plants and animals. Engineers play with physics and design; business people play with economics and human psychology.

Play leads to new discoveries and new solutions to old problems, and to happy, healthy individuals who enjoy their work. So stand back, get out of the way, and let your children play.

Q. What about socialization and social activities?

A. Homeschooling gives your child an opportunity to develop real socialization skills. Spending fifty percent of your waking hours with 30 children the same age is not real socialization. You may even avoid stereotyping, labeling, humiliation, designer jeans, and undue pressure concerning cliques, drugs, and sex.

By homeschooling, your children will have opportunities to learn, work, and play with children older and younger than themselves, and with adults. You may have to work at finding people, but it is generally not hard once you get started. You may have to be willing to drive farther than you really want, but you might find that you have more social opportunities than you can manage. Many homeschoolers find that they have to cut back on the social schedule to have time at home alone.

Children who have been schooled previously will have to redefine what friends are — generally homeschoolers have one or two really close friends they see regularly and a handful or two of acquaintances they enjoy on occasion. Do you have more than that?

The more you homeschool, the more homeschooling friends you will find. In many areas throughout the state there are formal or not so formal homeschool support groups that offer many opportunities to meet other children and provide time for socialization. Friendships no longer need to be limited to children of similar ages.

Homeschooling may provide an opportunity for siblings to improve their relationships with each other and for you to become friends with your children. Your child will have time for sports activities, musical groups, church and youth organizations, field trips, volunteer opportunities, arts and crafts workshops, neighborhood children's activities, story times at the local library, community drama groups and more. Homeschooling provides time for family support of critical areas of social development: love, self-discipline, security, interdependence, independence, and responsible use of freedom.

Q. How can I find homeschoolers in my community?

A. Information on contacting support groups is listed in Chapter 12, along with ideas on how to connect with other homeschoolers in your community. If you can't find a group in your area, a statewide homeschooling organization may be able to help you.

Q. How will I know if my child is keeping up with the other children her age?

A. This question arises from the belief that there is a proper scope and sequence of curriculum presentations, since public schools teach that way. For example, it is widely believed that children must read before they write, and that they must learn multiplication before division, but after addition. These beliefs are myths. Many children write and even spell before they read. Children learn to read as early as toddlerhood, or as late as their early teens. It makes no difference in the end. Some refuse to pick up a pencil and learn to write for many years, only to later develop a keen interest in calligraphy, creative writing, or journalism. Homeschooled children have broken all the school rules about "how children should be taught and how children learn" and will continue to break the rules.

Why do we as parents care if our children are "keeping up" with their age mates? Why do we need to compare? Learning academics is best treated with the same respect as learning to walk, or talk, or potty train. When the child is ready he will do it, and you won't be able to stop him from learning what he wants to know faster than you thought it could be learned. The goal is to learn the material, not to be the first to reach certain sign posts along the way.

"Keeping up" may not be a big issue unless you are homeschooling your child only temporarily. A curriculum guide and the annual, state-required testing can provide enough reassurance of satisfactory progress for most families. Otherwise, sit back and enjoy learning with your children, and worry a little less about which neighborhood child gets her multiplication tables memorized first.

Q. Can you use public school resources, take classes or play in school sports?

A. Schools are required to permit homeschooled children to participate in interscholastic activities such as sports or debate club, if the child meets certain requirements. For more information, see Chapter 2 and Appendix A.

Schools are not required by law to permit homeschooled students access to any other part of their program. Although it is rare, some districts do allow use of books and facilities, and permit students to participate in classes part-time. Contact your local school to see what possibilities there are.

Q. Can I homeschool my handicapped or learning disabled child?

A. Yes, it is legal in Oregon to homeschool your child if he has a handicap. Depending on the handicap, the state is even required by federal law to provide support for you. Your child must undergo testing, but after that stage, you can generally have as much or as little assistance as you want. Chapter 2 and Appendix A have more information. Contact the Department of Education (page 93) or your county's Education Service District (Appendix B) for more information.

Q. How can I make my child learn?

A. Making a child learn is a bit like making him eat ice cream. Offer ice cream as a treat from time to time, and she will lap it up. But if she has been spoon fed ice cream all her life on a strict schedule, she may need to avoid ice cream for a time before she remembers that she really does like it. Just so with learning. The best you can do is to create an environment that encourages learning and to demonstrate good learning practices yourself. If you are absolutely sure that your children must be forced to learn, you might prefer to find a compatible school and let someone else be the teacher. Your relationship with your child is too important to jeopardize with teacher/student conflicts.

Q. What do I do when my child complains that he is bored?

A. "Mom, I'm bored!" can usually be interpreted to mean, "Mom, entertain me!" Try suggesting a few activities the child can do alone or together with you. Sometimes this approach fails, and the responsibility for being bored can be left with the child: "Oh, you really are bored. That usually means that the next thing you do will be something really creative." And usually, that is just what happens.

Q. How do I find time to homeschool my children?

A. Homeschooling may not be as time-consuming as you might think.

In the first place, it does not take six hours a day to do the same amount of learning that takes place in six hours of school, even with the most structured and exacting curriculum. Learning can easily take place throughout the day at times that are otherwise wasted — in the car, for example. Mealtime and bedtime are other natural learning times for families with young children.

Second, children who learn at home are often more pleasant to be around than children who have struggled through a demeaning, exhausting day at school. Instead of trying to help cranky irritable children complete their homework, you can work with them when they are cheerful and fresh. You can allow them to play, eat, learn, and sleep on their own individual schedules or a schedule that works for your family.

Third, homeschooling gives families an opportunity to rearrange their lifestyles to suit the individual members. Taking personal responsibility for your children's education gives you a chance to take life at a slower or faster pace, if you wish. The whole family can hop out of bed at the crack of dawn to go fishing, or sleep late and do math in the Cheerios all morning. The children will learn in either case.

It is important for you, the homeschooling parent, to find time for yourself. Take an hour early in the morning, late at night, or ask your spouse to support you with an evening out or day off each week. You might try trading with another homeschooling parent once a week.

All of our lives are busy and homeschooling does add another dimension. Once you start homeschooling you will find your own schedule. Remember that cleaning, cooking, and shopping can all be valuable learning experiences, too.

Q. My children have been in school since kindergarten. Will they have a hard time adjusting?

A. This is a purely individual issue. Sometimes students who were very rebellious in school all along and really want to leave school adjust easily. Generally, students who did well and learned to please the teacher have a harder time adjusting. These students have to relearn learning for themselves. They must discover for themselves that learning is more than turning to page 22 and doing the problems.

Some people believe that it could take as long to adjust to homeschooling as the child has spent in school. It can be months or even a year or more for some children to adjust.

Major breakthroughs may occur when the child becomes so bored, so extremely bored, that she draws on some inner strength and breaks out on her own. Children have done nothing but read for months, or sit for weeks shooting rubber bands against the wall. Finally something clicks, and they are off and running.

Q. My child doesn't want to be homeschooled, but I think it would be best for her. How can I resolve this issue?

A. See next question.

Q. My child would love to be homeschooled, but I don't really think that I can do it. How can I resolve this issue?

A. Sorry, there are no easy answers. Talk to many different homeschooling families and read books and stories of what other families have done. Learn as much as you can and then consider the key issue: what is best for this child?

Exploring the facts may help you to find an acceptable resolution. Children who resist homeschooling, for example, may be afraid that they will have no friends, or lose all the friends they now have. They may be worried that their parents don't know enough to teach them, and need reassurance. They may worry about falling behind their classmates.

Parents who don't want to homeschool often worry about the extra time that homeschooling takes. They may lack the confidence in their ability to facilitate learning. Often friends, family, and neighbors put enormous pressure on parents to keep their child in school at all costs. Sometimes the parents disagree with each other about the proper path to take in a child's education. Parents are sometimes afraid that their children won't learn unless forced, or that the parent/child relationship would be jeopardized.

In any case, if you decide to try homeschooling, take it slowly. Perhaps a half time arrangement with the school can solve the problem. Get lots of support to help ease the transition. Cooperative homeschooling, community classes, and sports activities can ease the family into a new lifestyle.

Be willing to change your plans. Don't worry too much if homeschooling doesn't work out exactly as you expected. The key to success is patience and finding a balance that works for both you and your child. If your child is active and involved in life, you are probably highly successful, no matter what your expectations originally were.

Try homeschooling for a year, and if it doesn't work out, try plan B. Even if the child does nothing academic at all for the entire year, she will probably have little trouble catching up to the level of her former classmates. She may even be ahead of where she would have been. A year of freedom can cause much healing. Don't be afraid to try homeschooling again later.

If you have a teenager, give her a copy of *The Teenage Liberation Handbook*.

Q. Where do I get materials?

A. Lots of places: book stores, toy stores, garage sales, art stores, scientific equipment supply houses, friends, relatives, teacher supply houses like Learning World, your recycling, the woods, mail-order magazines, Goodwill. Part Three lists many resources for materials, and should get you started. Chapter 11 lists books that are stuffed with ideas and resources that are beyond the scope of this book. Once you start homeschooling you will develop an eye for useful or potentially useful items.

Try not to spend too much money on big expensive items unless you want them to be lasting, long term investments for your home. Looking through magazines and catalogs is a good way to see what type of "educational materials" are available. Choose prudently. If possible, play the game or read the book, or a least check the return policy before purchasing. Don't underestimate the power of the library. Ask for a library tour. You may be surprised by what is available to you at no cost.

If you feel you want help in finding materials, several consultants and planning services are available to help you individualize your child's program. A number of prepared curriculums are also available, and several are listed in Chapters 13 and 14.

Q. Do homeschoolers ever burn out?

A. Oh, yes. Both parents and children sometimes burnout. While the causes are many, the most common cause of burnout is too much structure. Families who want structured homeschooling should read *Homeschool Burnout* by Raymond and Dorothy Moore. Chapter 4 may also help you find a practical homeschooling structure that will help avoid burnout.

Trying to be super-homeschooler is another cause of burnout. When parents discover what their children have been missing out on by being in school, they race around trying to do it all. Such frantic behavior may even burn the children out long before the parents wear down. Remember that a part of being a good parent (or homeschooler) may include wanting to give them everything. But **being** a good parent (or homeschooler) requires that parents control that impulse and come to healthy decisions about what they will and will not do/buy/view/visit /feed/study/etc. Including the children in making such decisions, incidentally, is a key to involving children in understanding their family's value system.

Q. Can I work and homeschool?

A. Although most home educators do not work outside the home, two income families and working single homeschooling parents are increasing. Some parents have been lucky and have found places to work that welcome their children. Other people work out of their homes, or work split shifts or part-time, providing time for each parent to share in homeschooling. Care can be provided by a friend, relative, other homeschooling parent, or school.

If you choose to work, scheduling is very important. Let your children know when you can be completely theirs, then take the phone off the hook, and really spend some time with them. Some people, particularly those with younger children, prefer working part of the day, say the morning, then spending the afternoon with their children. Others feel that they need to have whole days to focus on either work or homeschooling. This is particularly true with families with older children who are taking trips or working on extended projects. For some families, it works for one parent to be home during the day and the other to be with the children on evenings and weekends. Experiment with what works best for your family.

Q. What is cooperative homeschooling?

A. The term *cooperative homeschooling* describes families who homeschool together in some form or another. Sometimes it simply refers to a parent-sharing arrangement. For example, one parent takes the children from both families Tuesday and the other takes them Thursdays. Some families share responsibilities according to age. One family takes all the younger children for the day, while the other offers a special activity for the older children.

Cooperative homeschooling also refers to a type of mini-school. Families may get together one or more days a week to share activities, parent skills, and social interaction. These gatherings may be free-form or very structured. Although several such arrangements have been truly wonderful, please heed one word of caution: It can be very disconcerting to both the children and the adults when one or more families leaves the group. Your homeschooling efforts may be disrupted. Do not become too dependent on anyone else for your homeschooling.

Q. What about missing the high school graduation ceremony or the prom?

A. Adults usually ask this question, not children. Once children start homeschooling, for the most part school and the rituals that go with it no longer concern them. They have real life at their hands.

If you want to have a graduation ceremony for your child, go right ahead and have one. You can rent gowns, a hall, have speakers, a formal dinner and dance, let children give performances or speak about their accomplishments - whatever you want. If you want to organize such an event and invite others to participate, statewide and local homeschooling newsletters are generally happy to publish such an announcement.

Better yet, why not create a new kind of graduation ceremony that is consistent with the kind of education your children are receiving, and truly celebrate young people's passage into adulthood with all the pomp and circumstance you can muster?

If your child takes the GED, some schools will allow her to participate in their local high school graduation ceremony. As for attending the prom, perhaps your child can find a schooled friend with whom he can attend.

Q. What about correspondence schools?

A. There are several good support schools throughout the country, though there are often better ways to use your money. But if you decide you would be more comfortable having correspondence school support, write to several schools to get an idea of what services are available, and for what price. Some schools are willing to put you in contact with other people in your state who are enrolled in their program, so you can get their opinion of the program.

In one program or another you can get teacher support, evaluation assessments, packaged curriculums, help with designing your own curriculum, people to deal with school district officials, diplomas, etc.

Q. What about college?

A. Yes, your children can go to college if they are homeschooled. And, no, they do not need to have a high school diploma to do so. Most colleges and universities require SAT scores or other entrance exams and many place even more weight on a person's individual ability and aptitude. Over one hundred schools do not require SAT scores. I know of at least one homeschooled student who has enrolled in an advanced math class at University of Oregon as a special student at age fourteen. (See Chapters 9 and 14 for more information about homeschooling teens.) Homeschooled students are welcomed in many institutions of higher learning throughout the country, ranging from local community colleges to Ivy League universities. If you are interested in attending a particular college or university, call the school's admissions department and ask about their policy for admitting homeschooled students.

Education is too important
to be left solely to the educators.

—FRANCIS KEPPEL

CHAPTER 2

Understanding Oregon's Homeschool Law

For many years Oregon lacked a homeschooling law. Families who wished to homeschool generally registered as private schools or worked with the local school district. This practice lead to unequal treatment of homeschooling families depending on which school district they resided in.

In an effort to equalize treatment, the Parent's Education Association (a fundamentalist Christian home education political action committee), introduced a homeschool bill. After much negotiation, the bill passed and continues to be Oregon's homeschool law.

Briefly, the law, O.R.S. 339.030 and its accompanying regulations, requires that homeschoolers notify their Education Service District that they intend to homeschool and that each child must be tested once a year. Children falling below the fifteenth percentile are required to enroll in school or to be supervised by a certified teacher.

Note: I have attempted to provide an overview of the basics of the homeschool law and its history. Each parent should read and be familiar with the law and regulations. See Appendix A for the full text. The law and its regulations are subject to change at any time. To be sure of the law consult the Department of Education or your attorney.

❖

Attempts to Change the Law

In 1990, Measure 11, a school choice referendum, was placed on the ballot. Measure 11 would have permitted parents to choose the school they wanted, private, public or homeschool. Parents would have received a $2,500 tax credit to support their choice.

The Oregon Board of Education was upset by this measure, and, in the Fall of 1990, moved to tighten Oregon's homeschooling law. The Board's efforts were rash and not well thought out. One proposal would have required children to attend school if they scored at the ninety-fifth percentile on their annual test one year and then dropped to the ninetieth percentile the next year. Due to an outpouring of opposition by homeschoolers, and the defeat of Measure 11, the Board tabled the proposed regulations.

In the Spring of 1991, the Parents Education Association, along with OCEAN (Oregon Christian Home Education Association Network), introduced a new bill that would have made the current regulations (testing at the fifteenth percentile or above) law, and therefore would not be subject to potential change by the Board of Education. It also provided that children not making satisfactory progress (scoring below the fifteenth percentile) could work with a certified teacher instead of attending school.

Although this bill passed the House unanimously and the Senate with only four opposing votes, the Governor vetoed the bill since it restricted state power over homeschooling. (During the summer of 1992, the Board amended the regulations to permit the certified teacher option.)

Also in 1991, a Eugene homeschooling family sponsored a bill to allow homeschool children to participate in public school interscholastic activities. This bill passed (see below).

Benefits of Oregon's Homeschool Law

Compared to many other states, Oregon is thought to have one of the better home education laws. Here are some of the benefits:

- Homeschoolers do not need the permission of the state to homeschool, and there are no restrictions on which families are allowed to homeschool, i.e., no requirement for parents to be college graduates, hold teaching certificates, or pass competency exams.

- Homeschoolers do not have to deal with individual schools or school districts. All correspondence is sent to your county Education Service District.

- Parents are free to choose their own curriculum. Educational goals and objectives do not need to be reviewed or approved by the state.

- Disputes between homeschooling families and public school officials cannot affect your right to homeschool. Students can only be sent to school for "unsatisfactory progress" on the annual test.

- Homeschooling students are evaluated objectively using a standardized test. In addition, a "passage rate" of scoring at or above the fifteenth percentile is considered reasonable. This is the same score required of students taking the GED.

- Homeschool students not making "satisfactory progress" are not required to attend public school; they may enroll in a private school of their choice, or work with a certified teacher.

- Parents may select one of several versions of seven different standardized tests. Parents may use the qualified tester of their choice and have the test administered at a site of their own choosing.

- Parents who do not to comply with the law are not threatened by the fear that the state will take away their children. Parents convicted of a violation of the homeschool statute are subject to a fine of not more than $100.

- Students are permitted to participate in public school interscholastic activities if they score at or above the twenty-third percentile on their annual test.

Detriments of Oregon's Homeschool Law

Many homeschoolers find Oregon's law unsatisfactory. Here are some detriments of the law:

- Due to testing and notification requirements, homeschoolers are subject to the scrutiny of "big brother." The complete freedom to educate one's own children has been taken away.

- Parents do not get any educational support for their tax dollars. Parents must even pay for the test the state requires their children to take.

- Families who would like to receive some services or materials from the public school system are denied access or are subject to the whims of public school officials.

- Children are subjected to the drawbacks of standardized testing.

- Although the law gives a choice of seven different tests, many of these tests are not available, due to tight test company restrictions on tester qualifications and restrictions on administering tests to homeschooled children. The cost testers must pay to acquire tests can be prohibitive.

- Children who do not make "satisfactory progress" must attend school, or be taught by a certified teacher.

- Children scoring below the twenty-third percentile are denied access to public school interscholastic activities.

- Parents who oppose testing have no alternative but to not comply with the law, subjecting them to possible invasion of privacy, as well as a fine.

Time Requirements For Notification

Families begin to comply with the homeschool law when the children are seven years of age. If your child is age seven or older before the beginning of the school year, you must send a letter of notification to the superintendent of your local ESD at least ten days before the first day of school. (A list of the ESD's is found in Appendix B.) However, if your child has not turned seven by the first day of school, she or he does not yet fall under the compulsory attendance law and notification is not required until the next school year.

If children aged seven or older are enrolled in private or public school at the time a decision to homeschool is made, a letter of notification to the superintendent of the ESD must be sent at least ten days before the intended date of withdrawal. Each year after that, notification must be sent to the superintendent of the local ESD ten days before the first day of school.

Specific Notification Requirements

Although some districts provide forms, the law requires that you send the superintendent of your ESD only a short letter with a few pieces of information:

- The child's and parent's name, address and phone number;
- The child's birth date;
- The public school district in which the family resides or the name of the school last attended.

Your local ESD must acknowledge receipt of the notification within 10 days.

Test Deadlines and Scores

The next step is to have your child tested. Parents may arrange to have their children tested by a state approved tester, or in their local public school, if the school grants permission. The state publishes a list of approved testers each year. Parents also have a choice of which test they want to have their children take, although most testers have access to only one or two tests. Lists of tests and test administrators are listed in Appendix C and Appendix D.)

If you send notification to the ESD before school starts, your child's initial scores must be submitted to the ESD on or before October 31. If your child is withdrawn from school during the school year, his initial score must be submitted to your local ESD within eight weeks of the notification.

The Board of Education permits tests administered and scored after March 1 to be submitted in the fall to fulfill the requirements of the law. If your child's initial test was administered on or after March 1, that test score may be submitted as both the initial reporting requirement and the fall (October 31) requirement. Thereafter, the child may be tested at any time between March 1 and October 31.

The initial test score is the standard by which next year's test will be judged. It does not make any difference what test score your child receives the first year. A child cannot be sent to school based on the first set of test scores, so you have at least one year of unrestricted homeschooling.

A student is considered to have made "satisfactory progress" if she or he scores at or above the fifteenth percentile, or the student's score is equal to or greater than the score he or she had on the previous year's test. In other words, when students score at or above the fifteenth percentile, they are fine. However, if a child scores at the seventh percentile, the next year that child must score at or above the seventh percentile.

The percentile rating is not the number of questions the child gets correct on a test, but her standing in comparison to a "norming" group, a statistical sampling of students who have taken the same test. For example, if a child scores at the eightieth percentile, that means that for every one hundred students that participated in the test company's norming test group, eighty students got fewer answers correct than your child did. Your test administrator will score the test and tell you in what percentile your child scored.

Interscholastic Activities Law

The Interscholastic Activities Law allows homeschooled students to participate in public or private school activities such as athletics, music, speech and similar activities. An activity that culminates in competition between schools is considered an interscholastic activity.

A homeschool student who wants to participate in interscholastic activities in the district in which he resides must:

- Fulfill the regular homeschool law requirements;

- Score no less than the twenty-third percentile on the annual standardized test;

- Meet the other school requirements placed on children participating in the activity, except for class attendance requirements; and

- Submit the student's test scores to the school district of residence before participation in the activity.

Immunization

When you register with your ESD, they may send you information on immunizations. Homeschoolers are not required to be immunized nor are they required to complete an immunization form unless they are attending school part-time or participating in interscholastic activities. You can get an immunization form at your neighborhood school.

GED (General Educational Development)

Homeschooled students are permitted to take the GED at age sixteen if they are both in compliance with the homeschool law and making satisfactory progress. Your letter from the local ESD is submitted as evidence of compliance.

High School Diplomas

If a homeschooler plans to enter or return to high school to receive a diploma, talk to the principal as soon as the student is enrolled. Request that the school evaluate your credits and the number of years of school attendance, or equivalent, and that they inform you of which competencies you must demonstrate to meet the graduation requirements. (See OAR 581-22-717)

Be prepared to document "credits," since credits are the basis of the graduation requirements. Unschoolers may need to be creative, i.e., document books used, experiences, projects, time spent. To graduate, a student must earn a minimum of 22 credits: language arts, 3; mathematics, 2; science, 2; U. S. history, 1; global studies, 1;

government, 1/2; health education, 1; physical education, 1; career development, 1/2; personal finance and economics, 1; applied arts, fine arts, or foreign language, 1. (See OAR 581-22-316) Make sure that you receive a reply in writing and work out any problems early.

Alternative Education Options

If your child has been truant from school, i.e., not complying with the homeschool law, for six months or more, he may be eligible for certain alternative education programs or services from the local ESD. Services may include tutors, participating in classes at local schools, books and supplies, etc. For more information, contact the local ESD.

Challenged or Handicapped Homeschoolers

Children who have a mental or physical handicap may be homeschooled. They must either fulfill the regular compliance rules as stated above, or work with the local school district of residence to design an IEP (Individualized Education Plan.) For further information, contact the local school district or the Department of Education. See Appendix A, Chapter 11 for books on homeschooling challenged students, and contact NATHHAN (page 102).

CHAPTER 3

Selecting A Test Administrator

When it is time to have your child tested, you must choose an approved test and a state qualified tester. The approved tests are listed in Appendix C and the qualified testers are in Appendix D. The Department of Education or your county's Education Service District(Appendix B) can provide you with an updated list if necessary. Qualified testers are generally certified teachers, but there are several ways to become a tester. Read the homeschooling law and regulations in Appendix A. You can choose any person on the list, or who is otherwise approved by the Department of Education, so long as the tester is not related to the child by blood or marriage.

Besides choosing a test administrator who is qualified, there are a number of points that you might consider as you select the test and tester that are right for your child.

First, what tests does the tester offer? Can you preview the tests in order to determine the most appropriate test for your child? Most testers offer only one or two choices, but be sure to ask. Find out if the tester offers study guides for the test you have chosen, or if she or he knows where to get the guides. Taking a practice test can be helpful in preparing a child with the test taking skills needed for success.

Second, do you want individual or group testing? If cost is a concern, and you feel a group test setting will not adversely affect your child's success, you might consider a group test. You can check with your local school district and find out if you can have your child tested in one of the neighborhood schools during their regular testing sessions. If you prefer a private tester, you may still be able to arrange for a group setting. Be sure to ask. You may be able to arrange group testing in your home for a small group of children from your support group.

You may prefer to have your child tested individually. Some testers are willing to come to your home. Do you want to have your child tested at home in his usual learning environment, or are you willing to go elsewhere for the test?

If you want the testing to take place in your home, can you find a tester who agrees to this arrangement? Can you provide a quiet, interruption-free environment? Your home is usually the best, most natural environment for testing, but if you are in the middle of a remodeling project, other arrangements should probably by made.

If you decide to go outside your home for the test, what are the testing conditions that you prefer? You might consider the general comfort of the room used for testing: lighting, room temperature, ambient noise level, table and chair size.

Third, what are the rules of the testing? Are the directions read aloud? How are questions handled? Can a parent be present in the room? How many breaks are there? How long are the breaks? Is there a place to run off steam, use the bathroom, and to eat or drink something while taking a break?

Fourth, if your child has special testing needs, make sure those can be accommodated. For example, if your child is allergic to cats, you will want to make sure there will be no cats present during the testing time.

Finally, how do you feel about the tester? Is she or he generally warm and supportive? What are the tester's attitudes towards the test? Does the tester hold an attitude that might limit your child's ability to perform to the best of his or her ability? Does she or he relieve test anxiety or add to it?

Choosing a test administrator is subjective, and there is no perfect tester for everyone. A tester who is calming to one child can cause anxiety in another child. If you are at all uncertain, either about the tester or the testing environment, a brief personal visit can go a long way towards alleviating concern. You may want to meet one or two testers and see the testing environment before making a final selection.

Your child may be anxious about the test, or maybe Mom and Dad are worried about their child's ability to be successful. The best way to assure success is for the child to view the testing situation as a game to be played. The testing game should be played hard and seriously, but it is just a game, after all. Ideally, the attitudes of both the parents and the test administrator, along with the testing environment, should create an atmosphere in which the child can do his or her very best.

❖ ❖ ❖

CHAPTER 4
Finding Your Family's Homeschooling Style

The more homeschooling families you meet, the more you will notice that there are as many homeschooling styles as there are homeschooling families! Each child has a learning style that includes her unique personality, interests, and learning methods. A family's homeschooling style must be flexible enough to allow for the learning styles and interests of each member of the family.

Some families choose a highly structured program, styled after conventional schools Others, rejecting this more structured format, allow their children unlimited freedom from external structure. Many homeschoolers vacillate between the two extremes. They flounder about from too structured to too relaxed until, eventually, they find a style that suits them. Unfortunately, many families burn out on homeschooling before they find their own homeschooling style, without even giving it a fair try.

Avoiding Homeschool Burnout

It is natural for people to think of homeschooling in the light of their personal public or private schooling experience. Textbooks, six hour days, same age groupings, teacher-directed learning activities, schedules, desks, lectures, and tests are some conventional trappings of schooling that parents remember from their childhood.

It may seem best and easiest to the new homeschooler to take these and other elements of conventional group learning and transplant them into the homeschool.

However, transporting traditional schooling into a homeschool does not guarantee success. It may in fact be disastrous. Most veteran homeschoolers will agree that trying to imitate schools in the home is a leading cause of homeschool burnout. At the very least, important opportunities may be missed when homeschools duplicate conventional school techniques too closely.

Homeschooling is not a method of cramming learning into kids' heads. Homeschooling is not a way of forcing children to learn, a shortcut to straight "A's," or a device for protecting children from the serious social problems of today's society. Homeschooling is not a set of books, a daily schedule, or some clever tricks for managing child behavior.

At its best, homeschooling is a way of life, a distinctly unique method of educating children. It offers opportunities and challenges that do not relate in any way to the typical schooling experience that most of us remember from childhood. Homeschooling families live a lifestyle that is unique in the community.

Homeschooling places full responsibility for the education of the children on the family. With this responsibility comes freedom— freedom to tailor education to the individual needs of each child.

Learning opportunities become readily available through homeschooling that are next to impossible to achieve in a traditional school setting. One-on-one learning can be the norm instead of the exception. Learning, or teachable, moments that occur during the normal course of the day can be seized as they arise, rather than scheduled into next week's lesson plans. Learning activities can be casually scheduled into the flow of other family activities, instead of strictly scheduled for bureaucratic convenience.

Families who do not find a balanced homeschooling style that satisfies the needs of both parents and children often give up on homeschooling. To help you avoid burning out before discovering the full potential of homeschooling, explore a wide variety of homeschool styles.

Style and Structure Must Benefit All Family Members

One child in a family may require lots of attention and support, even hand holding, when taking on a new learning project. Yet the same child may hang on to a project until it reaches some level of perfection that pleases her.

Another child may rarely take an interest in anything that is easy for her. Instead she thrives when she finds challenges that push her to the very limits of her capabilities. Only when she struggles and finally grasps a difficult idea, she is satisfied. These two children have remarkably different learning styles, and yet, the home-school setting must include support and challenge for each child.

Children learn in a variety of ways and on vastly different schedules. One child in a family may be an early reader, while another doesn't make sense of print until much older. The homeschool environment is flexible enough that consideration for the uniqueness of each child's learning styles and preferences is not a hardship but an opportunity.

Creative solutions are often necessary. For instance, if one child is allergic to animals, and another loves and needs pets to care for, what unique solutions can the family develop to meet the needs of both children?

The personal style of the homeschooling parent must be considered as well. What do you enjoy? How can you incorporate meeting the children's learning needs into your daily routine? Which subjects do you love or hate? When do you have the most patience? Do you enjoy big messy projects, or do you prefer more structured activities? *How will you make time for yourself?*

Many homeschooling parents take the opportunity to learn something new themselves. Your kids will love you for it! They will be your greatest advocates as you struggle to learn and you will become more understanding of the difficulties that your children encounter in their learning activities. You will gain insight into your personal learning style and the ways you incorporate new learning into your life.

Getting Started

How, then, do you discover your family's homeschooling style or styles? Simply begin. Don't wait for the perfect time, or until you've read all the books, or until your mother approves. Try the ideas you have, the ones you remember from teachers you loved, the ideas you always wanted to try but never had the chance. Learn French, climb a mountain, read the encyclopedia, build a waterfall. In other words, if you have ideas about how you might begin to homeschool, then begin. Your homeschooling style will begin to show itself along the way.

If you feel unsure of yourself and don't know how to begin, there are several possibilities for gaining some ideas.

First, you could get a curriculum guide or even a full curriculum. Use it with the children if you want and if they are agreeable, or just use it as a guide to give you some ideas of what can be learned at a particular age and ability level.

Another way to learn about how other families homeschool is to read several of the many homeschooling books now available. These books can help you get a sense of how different families' homeschooling styles changed and adapted as the children changed and grew. Read these books, not with an eye to duplicate the Colfax, Wallace, Barker, Moore, or Leistico homeschooling style in your home, but with an eye to seeing how other families have worked together to develop a homeschooling way of life.

A small word of caution here. There is a risk in reading those wonderful books. While the books offer encouragement and confidence that, yes, homeschooling really does work (just look at these wonderful families and their wonderful children!), these same books may discourage a shaky new (or veteran) homeschooler. It is tempting to compare our homeschooling lives with the lives of the "stars." We should be careful not to judge ourselves failures as homeschoolers if we haven't built telescopes, traveled abroad, raised sheep, or played concertos with our children.

I confess to moments of depression after reading the home-schooling story of another family, sorry to be reminded of the paths not taken. Remember, however, that each well-known family had doubts and fears along the way, too. They learned from their mistakes, and went on to greater successes. Each of us has a unique homeschooling story to tell, and these stories should remind us of the wonderfully diverse world we live in and the opportunities that can be created for families right where they live.

Finally, you could find out how other families homeschool by visiting with other homeschooling families. On the local level, you can find other homeschooling families through your support network. (See Chapter 12) How do they spend their days? What materials and resources do they use? A visit to a homeschooling family, or even a short phone call, can tell you a lot about whether this family's style will work for you. (Remember that other homeschoolers are busy people, too! Be respectful of their time and energy!)

Suppose you visit a family that has carefully scheduled study periods, a packaged curriculum, and a tidy and orderly study area. Would you and your children feel comfortable and relaxed, feeling that you could do this too? Or would you feel overwhelmed by the immensity of the task of providing daily instruction for your children in addition to your other daily tasks? Would your children enjoy this type of learning environment, or would there be a constant struggle to get them to do the required work?

Suppose you visit a different family, one that has Legos, animals, books, puzzles, microscopes, and many projects-in-progress scattered all over the house. Do you feel comfortable, knowing that you have walked into a rich learning environment, where children can easily learn all day long in a variety of ways? Or do you feel put off by or overwhelmed by the immensity of the task of keeping up with all this stuff in addition to your other daily tasks?

These are two examples of the many varied styles of homeschooling, all of which work successfully for different families. The children in each home learn and grow, and the parents find ways to balance the learning needs of their children with other demands on their time. However, a homeschooling style that works great in one family can drive another family crazy! There simply is no right, or only, way to homeschool. The method you choose should fit your family. You may want to experiment with several ideas before you decide what works best for you and your children.

Once you know how other families homeschool, take a good inventory of your own family. Individual tastes and differences, interests, values, and attitudes will affect the type of homeschool you have.

Are you urban, suburban, small town, or rural? A rural family and an urban family probably will have different resources and different needs. Are you well connected with other homeschooling families or are you isolated? Do you live in a neighborhood with lots of appropriate playmates, or will you need to work to create social opportunities for your children? Does your family like to spend quiet time at home with books, computers, art, music, craft and building projects, and games? Or do you prefer to get out in the community, going camping, socializing, taking classes, shopping, taking cultural trips, etc.? Will you need to budget carefully, or can you purchase resources more freely? (A helpful article on low-cost homeschooling is included in a pamphlet called *For New Homeschoolers*, Chapter 11.) How many children? Are some night owls and some early birds? What role will each parent play? What sacrifices may need to be made, if any? These are some of the considerations that you should take into account as you plan.

Along the Way—How Do I Know If It Is Working?

Just as parents know instinctively when their babies are tired, hungry, wet, or are willing to be held by strangers, parents usually know their children's learning needs best. They are often the first to know when something is or is not working in their child's life. Homeschooling requires this same "checking in." Some careful observations will tell you if your plan is working. Children have day-to-day problems like everyone else, yet, if you are observant, you can generally figure out when there is a trend to the positive or the negative.

Are the children usually happy, busy, engaged, enthusiastic, challenged, whether at play or at work? It's working, folks! Are they sullen, squabbling, always bored, negative, television-addicted, combative? Their behavior is always telling you something! If the behavior is more negative than positive for a period of time, it's time for Detective Dad or Mom to try to discover the source of the problem and to help the child find direction.

"But I can't read my children's minds! I don't know what they need!" I hear your cry, and I believe that you are actually asking, "How can I learn to be the best possible detective at identifying my children's learning needs?" Well, good parents, you already are the best! You are the best qualified people in the world to take an educated guess at how to meet your children's individual needs. You know the continuum of their lives, have shared their joys and sorrows, illness and growth spurts, successes and failures.

You were present when your children learned the momentous skills of walking and talking, and you encouraged all the practice that built up to mastering those skills. You supported and encouraged them. You instinctively understood each child's method of learning. You waited patiently, neither lecturing nor scolding, but giving the kind of help that each child asked for. If he wanted to hold your hand to practice those first few steps, you were there for him. If he wanted to do it his way, you stood back, watching and "being there." No child specialist or "expert" could have done it better. You bring those same skills with you as you support, encourage, and observe as your child tackles equally challenging and exciting endeavors. And still, no "expert" can do it better.

Don't get too comfortable, though, because once you finally do get things figured out, you can expect change before long. Growing children are changing children, and changing children need different things at different stages of life. Perhaps you will find that the structured curriculum you once loved is now too restrictive, or that the previously relaxed atmosphere, now filled with squabbling children, is driving you crazy! The structure you choose should enhance family life, not complicate it.

If the structured curriculum you loved last fall is now too restrictive, lay it aside for a time. Use the curriculum materials as a resource, a tool for learning, rather than as a way of life. If you never touch the thing again, consider it a well-learned lesson for your family.

Meanwhile, use the time you have gained to immerse yourself in the excitement and joy of your children's learning experiences. Look at bugs and try to identify them; ooh and aah at the sights seen under a microscope or through a telescope; study fish anatomy; enjoy a read-aloud marathon; do math problems on paper napkins at dinner; make up silly poems as you ride along in the car. You will be surprised at how much they are learning, even when days go by without a look at the curriculum.

On the other hand, your lives may need a bit more structure and order. Consider setting aside certain hours for particular tasks. You may decide to try a math program, a reading list, publishing a newsletter (guaranteed pressure!), piano lessons, a pet to care for, a scheduled weekly trip to the library, a regular household chore or two, or a scheduled day with other homeschooling friends. If setting aside certain hours for particular tasks brings peace and order out of the chaos, then establish a schedule and stick to it.

My daughter could not and would not tolerate traditional structured learning for many years. She now works in not only a structured math program, but an entire structured curriculum. And why not? She knows even better than anyone, at this stage in her life, what she needs. Yet it took several false starts, and much frustration, before she finally conveyed the message: "I want and am ready for rigorous, structured academics." Because she had been so "unstructure-able" when she was younger, it was difficult for her parents to realize that she was "movin' on . . ."

Choosing a structured curriculum does not mean that we have abandoned our previous homeschooling life style for a highly structured one. We still curl up together and read for long hours. We get together with other families frequently and take the classes and sports that she loves. We still do mental math for the fun of it. Instead of replacing any of these things, the curricular materials have become a tool in her Learner's Tool Kit. She uses the materials in her way, and at her pace. Yet even if she tires of using the structured program before completing it, she will have learned a great deal. She will know about the content of this program, about how structured programs work, and about how she responds to such programs.

Go Ahead—Jump Right In!

Don't be afraid to jump into the homeschooling waters with both feet! The secret of an effective homeschooling style is this: homeschooling is fun! Spend time with your children. Watch the light bulbs of inspiration and understanding go on in their minds.

Don't be afraid to change directions if the method you have chosen doesn't work. Try something else.

Don't worry too much about disrupting the children's learning processes with a mid-year change of program or curriculum. Life is full of change, and change always provides opportunities for growth and learning. Your children will benefit from your decision to keep searching for a style that works best for you.

You will know that you are finding your ideal homeschooling style when you relax and start to really have fun while you learn. There's nothing quite like the feeling of satisfaction and empowerment you get as you regain the personal responsibility for your family's education.

No student knows his subject:
the most he knows is where and how to find out
the things he does not know.
—WOODROW WILSON

CHAPTER 5

Curriculum Planning

Curriculum: what homeschoolers do all day. Whether your curriculum is interest-initiated, a traditional purchased academic course of study, or something between, your curriculum is what the children do and learn.

The richest "course of study" is to be found throughout our homes, our neighborhoods, and our communities. Access to a public library and creative use of the home and community resources are the basic ingredients of the best free education in the world. Beyond those basics there are many, many resources available. Oregon law neither requires nor recommends that you use a packaged curriculum. It is a decision you make individually.

You may want resources for designing your own curriculum, a packaged commercial curriculum, a correspondence school, a curriculum planning service, or access to materials for individualized planning. A good selection of resources and materials are listed in Part 3 of this book.

You might first ask yourself whether or not you need to purchase a packaged set of curricular materials. Packaged curriculums are very expensive. You might prefer to place your "curricular dollars" elsewhere. For example: a piano; gymnastics lessons; a huge Lego set; a set of Great Books; a set of encyclopedias; a $200 dictionary; the very best art supplies; a great set of hands-on math materials; a history trip to Washington, D. C.; microscopes and magnets; Spanish lessons; museum or zoo memberships; flying lessons; a computer; a beginning Reader Book Club membership; tools, nails, and lumber; bicycles for the whole family; or a trip around the state or the country or the world. Get the idea?

Commercial curriculum packages are a bit like TV dinners: convenient, tidy, and attractively packaged, but a bit dried out and bland on the inside. Generally, greater variety and appeal can be attained elsewhere at less expense. A curriculum may add an interesting dimension to a child's learning and can be quite convenient, but as a steady diet, beware. Bored, resigned, lackluster learners may result.

A packaged curriculum may actually interfere with children's natural learning processes. Remember that all commercial curriculums are a distillation of knowledge by strangers who do not know your child at all. Your child's learning style is unique, and no curriculum will ever be developed that will perfectly meet the needs of all children.

Finding Curriculum

Still, a packaged curriculum may be just right for you and your family at one time or another. Some children love working through a set of books. Some families prefer to follow a set curriculum, and others may use a structured curriculum after their children reach a particular age. You might choose to purchase a curriculum to help make the transition from public schooling to homeschooling. If you plan to homeschool only temporarily, a curriculum package may be the best choice.

Curriculums are available for purchase from a number of correspondence schools, private schools and academies, and certain other educational institutions. Some curriculums can be purchased with teacher assistance at an additional cost. Curriculum suppliers are listed in Chapters 13 and 14 , and Chapter 16 lists textbook representatives.

Homeschooling conferences and curriculum fairs, where you can view and purchase materials, are held in Oregon, Washington, and California. Used curriculum fairs are very popular, and are often held in conjunction with a conference, workshop, or curriculum fair. Check with regional and state networking organizations (OHEN, LIGHT, OCEAN, WHO, HSC, and others— see Chapter 12) to find out when and where these events take place.

Talk to other homeschoolers about what they have found to be useful. You might advertise for a curriculum in a homeschooling newsletter or magazine, if you know what you are looking for.

Some questions you might consider while you are looking for a curriculum include:

1. Are the materials adaptable to your child's style of learning?
2. Is the content interesting to both you and your child?
3. What, if any, values are taught in the curriculum?
4. Are the activities varied enough to interest your child, or do they depend heavily on filling in workbooks?
5. Can your older child use the curriculum somewhat independently, or will she be dependent on you to explain directions?
6. Are teachers' materials and answer keys included or can they be purchased separately? It would be a shame to buy a teachers' manual that only collected dust, if you really don't want it.

Before purchasing, shop around. Read the ads in homeschooling magazines. Ask other homeschoolers what they like and what they don't like. Send for some catalogs. Don't feel rushed to buy just anything simply because school starts tomorrow. Usually those who benefit the most from the hurried purchase of commercial curriculum materials are the writers, publishers, and sellers.

Try before you buy. Some curriculum suppliers sell a sample lesson at a nominal cost. Other suppliers may be willing to do the same if asked. Be sure to check out the company's refund and return policy for unused curriculum. Preview the material if possible.

Your child's love of learning will benefit more from carefully selected materials. Hasty selections can be expensive lessons—usually for Mom and Dad!

Expect to purchase some materials that you don't use, no matter how well you plan. All homeschooling families eventually buy some expensive dust collectors. You can't always predict your child's needs with complete accuracy, so chalk up those expensive purchases to experience. If you cannot return the materials, save them for the younger brother, sell them to another homeschooling family, or give them to a friend.

❖

Individualizing Curriculum

Many parents assume that the key to homeschool success is a good commercial curriculum. This assumption is understandable. Most public schools use expensive, carefully marketed, commercial curriculum packages. Parents are naturally led to assume that a commercial curriculum is the essential ingredient in education.

Planning your child's education individually may make you uncomfortable. "What if I don't cover the basics? What if my child can't get a job when he grows up?" It might be helpful to think briefly about school curriculums and knowledge.

Remember that a curriculum is a distillation of knowledge designed for a large audience. Curriculums are graded for particular age or ability levels, and they are designed to spiral. That is, each grade level covers similar material, with increasing difficulty and depth. Curriculum also reviews the previous years' material: up to ninety percent of the math curriculum in any given year is review.

A general, spiraling, graded curriculum is often inappropriate for individualized learning. For instance, one eleven year old child may be "ready" for her first structured curriculum at fifth grade, but she is most appropriately placed in seventh grade materials. Another eleven year old may be struggling with reading skills. She may need structured curriculum in math but not in "reading dependent" courses. Most children will not derive lasting benefit from structured programs until at least age ten or twelve. Many children will never benefit from a full-blown curriculum, but find such material restrictive and boring.

Purchased curriculums are tidy compact packages that require a minimum of involvement from the parent. There is little room in such packages to accommodate individual learning style variations, let alone individual interests. In today's literate, information-rich society, even the best commercial curriculum is just as likely to limit a child's education as it is to enhance it.

A great education can be had with no formal curriculum materials at all. A good education can be gotten because of the best curriculum materials or in spite of the worst.

If a curriculum cannot guarantee a good education, we must ask ourselves: What are the key elements in a child's life that result in a good education?

It is important to look beyond the surface trappings of education with which we are familiar. Consider which elements of life are necessary to a healthy and successful learning environment.

Many homeschooling parents look to their children for clues when they plan individual educational programs. They observe carefully to discover their children's learning styles, interests, natural talents, developmental stages, physical needs, and personalities.

Most parents find that, when they begin to trust themselves more than outside experts, they are keenly aware of their children's abilities and needs. Parents use their personal knowledge of their children to devise a learning plan that optimally meets the educational needs of each child. Expert advice, while sometimes helpful, should never replace parental judgment.

Remember that children whose parents guide them in following their interests do learn the basic subject areas. They simply follow a different time line and schedule than is normal in schools and traditional curricular materials.

The home and the community most naturally meet these basic educational needs. With the basic educational needs met, children will thrive, growing into healthy educated individuals, who can make their own decisions and live useful and meaningful lives.

Remember, too, that you have your own educational experiences to draw from, as well as your life as an adult and a parent. If you feel you need outside support in developing curriculum, there are many books and pamphlets available to help you. (An excellent resource is Rebecca Rupp's *Good Stuff: Learning Tools For All Ages*.) You might want to seek out a homeschooling consultant or curriculum planning service, correspondence school, or local teacher to lend you a hand.

In Part Three of this handbook you can find: subject area materials; local community resources, including retail, field trips, museums, points of interest; curriculum planners, homeschooling programs, and consultants who can help with your planning; textbook resources; pen pal and children's periodical lists; religious homeschooling resources and materials; and more.

Parents who prefer not to purchase a prepared curriculum might consider the following suggested components of a good basic education, before making any purchases.

❖

Learner's Tool Kit — Thirteen Suggestions

- **Positive adult role models**. Children need access to adults doing real things, running the gamut from scrubbing a floor to scrubbing a space mission, and anything between.

- **The opportunity to experience the world personally**, using hands, bodies, and all the senses, as well as the mind. These experiences could include water, sand, mud, plants, animals, cooking, repair, all aspects of family life, social relationships, privacy, books, art, construction, crafts, dance, model building, sports, drama, math, communication, machinery (including anything from crowbars to computers), music, science, spiritual beliefs, literature, history, travel, and more. Paper and pencil representations of reality (i.e. packaged curriculums or dependence on workbooks) are occasionally a valuable tool. Used excessively, such materials are a flavorless substitute for the real thing.

- **Access to adults who are interested in their [children's] questions and are willing to help them find answers and materials**. Knowing that questions and knowledge are important to a grown-up person helps children build confidence and knowledge in the best possible way.

- **Generous access to materials, books, and resources**. These do not have to be expensive, just plentiful. Use libraries, catalogs, garage sales, surplus stores, educational stores and catalogs, community resources, etc. Could your homeschooling group have a materials exchange?

- **Loving guidance in pursuing interests and developing a value system**. Homeschooled children easily develop self-discipline and desirable values with gentle, firm direction from parents.

- **The opportunity to take measured risks and to experience the consequences**. Risk-taking is not always thought of as a good thing, yet a life without some risk is stagnant. Knowing how to judge whether a risk is worth the price is a valuable life skill.

- **The opportunity to make many mistakes and to learn from them, with no threat of loss of self-esteem.** Don't we learn the most from our mistakes, so long as we aren't hassled too much for blowing it? Children deserve many early opportunities to do the same.

- **Contact with a diverse, multi-aged, group of children and adults from whom to choose playmates and friends.** Children need real life opportunities to learn how to get along with all kinds of people in many different circumstances.

- **Enough time to play and fantasize, both alone and with others.** It has often been said that play is the child's work.

- **Time and privacy for thinking, imagining, being bored, "down" time.** Most schooling strips children of privacy. Homeschooling should allow plenty of "alone time" opportunities. How important it is to learn to live with yourself just as you are! Homeschooling provides the freedom to discover your heart's desire in your own time and way!

- **Freedom from being compelled to learn a subject before readiness or interest has developed.** Compelled learning before readiness or interest are developed is a prime cause of children becoming labeled as learning disabled. Even worse, compelled learning causes children to develop a distaste for learning.

- **Opportunities to work and contribute to the world, both for financial gain, and in service to others.** The community, the family, and the child all benefit when opportunities to do meaningful work are made available to all children and teenagers.

- **Absolute assurance that they are loved and trusted.** The security that develops from feeling cared for and trusted lends courage for learning new and challenging things.

Example is not the main thing in life—
it is the only thing.
—ALBERT SCHWEITZER

CHAPTER 6

A Few Words About Words

Reading and writing are the key skills that unlock much other knowledge. Here are a few ideas for you to consider as you decide how to teach your children these important skills.

Teaching Children How to Read

Parents can set the stage for their children to learn to read in two important ways: 1) Reading to their children and enjoying books with them, and 2) Enjoying reading themselves. If children see their parents reading for pleasure and to gain information, they realize that reading is a worthwhile skill to master and will want to imitate them just as they did when they learned walking and talking.

If you read to your children regularly, the love and joy of books will follow. Your children will eventually want to be able to master this skill to avoid being dependent on others. Don't stop reading to your children when they begin to read on their own. In fact, family reading through adulthood can be a favorite family ritual.

Some children learn to read through writing, others learn by reading street signs, while others learn by memorizing the stories that are read to them. Some learn at age four and others at age ten. Some want mom or dad nearby every step of the way. Others go off and struggle through books on their own. Each child will find his own time and way. Your job is to share your love of reading and to be there to help. The child will do the rest.

A battle about just how to teach reading has raged for many years in the education community, and that battle has spilled over into the homeschooling community. Some say phonics is the only way to teach reading, while others contend that whole language is the only answer.

The "phonics camp" teaches children the sounds and word attack skills, and generally provides reading material with a limited vocabulary for the child to practice his decoding skills.

The "whole language camp" declares phonics to be one of three useful reading strategies, the other two being the use of semantics (what makes sense) and syntax (what sounds right grammatically). Whole language teachers use literature and a wide base of reading material. While they usually suggest teaching all reading strategies equally, whole language advocates are often perceived to be against phonics instruction.

As homeschooling parents, we can offer all the strategies we know of to help youngsters who are learning to read, and leave the arguments behind. The goal of any reading instruction should be for children to learn to read, not to use or prove a particular method of instruction.

It makes sense for children to have as many strategies as possible when they begin to read. One strategy may seem more natural for a child at one developmental stage or another in his learning career.

Try to emphasize the pleasure of reading, the fascinating stories, interesting ideas, and useful information that can be found in books and other printed matter. Then, when you feel instruction is needed, make your lessons short, to the point, and as unobtrusive as you possibly can, and get on with the story!

Phonics

You probably don't need to buy a phonics program unless you yourself do not know basic phonics. Generally, children do not need a separate phonics program if they can sit by their parents and get the tips they need as they read together.

Some children who learn to read on their own through writing may in fact be designing their own personalized phonics program.

Suppose your child is just learning to write letters. "Mommy, how do you spell CAT?" "Let me think," says Mom. "You want to spell CAT. 'K-k-k' is the first sound. In this word we spell that sound with the letter 'c.' Write c. 'A-a-a' comes next. Write the letter 'a.' 'T-t-t' is spelled with the letter 't.' There, you have written CAT. May I read the word you wrote?" In this example Mom is thinking out loud and her child can observe the process.

When a child is a little older, you will want to encourage him to figure out what he already knows about the word. He may know that CAT begins with the 'k-k-k' sound, but he may be unsure whether it is spelled with 'c' or 'k.' Most of the time, though, parents just give the information requested, and the child will develop his own strategies naturally. Your child will give you clues as to how much information he wants.

Correcting Oral Reading

If you have been reading books and stories aloud to your child, he already knows that reading is supposed to make sense. *This knowledge is an important key to learning to read, and you should take advantage of it.* (If you ever suspect that your child reads without understanding what he is reading, stop all reading instruction and get back to the basics: reading and talking about reading—together!)

One rule of thumb is not to make corrections unless asked. If the story makes sense, who cares whether the child reads "him" or "them"? When the child pauses to study a word, stay quiet and allow him to think it though. He will probably use grammatic and contextual clues without you suggesting them. He will make his own corrections or ask for help when what he has read doesn't make sense.

When asked for help you need to decide what type of help to give. Usually your child will give you clues as to what kind of help he wants. If he is caught up in the middle of an exciting story, he probably doesn't really want a phonics lesson. You may just want to say what the word is that he is having difficulty with. This method helps maintain the integrity of a story and disturbs comprehension the least.

If you suspect that your child is not using all the strategies available, by all means take some time to talk about different ways of figuring out words. Just try not to do it in the middle of the first reading of a story.

Help your child to use all the information available on the page. You might suggest that he try to get a clue about a difficult word by trying to figure out what would make the sentence meaningful (semantics) or grammatically correct (syntax). It can be helpful to guess what the word might be from the story line, the make up of the sentence or paragraph, or from the picture (predicting). A good reader will use all of these tools.

A good time to help your child learn sound/symbol relationships is when he is trying to figure out the words on the cereal box, street signs, or other real print that has limited meaning. You could provide information about the sounds or offer helpful rules.

A favorite activity in our family has been to read magazines and newspaper headlines with young children, looking at and discussing pictures, and figuring out words together. Many of our so-called phonics lessons were in the car reading signs as we traveled down the highway. That way, we got to talk about the sounds of letters without interrupting the flow of a good story.

Types Of Books

There are so many kinds of books! Make regular trips to the library and select a variety. When visiting a book store, try to read the entire book before purchasing it. Choose works with stories you enjoy that have pleasing illustrations. It can become a challenge if your child falls in love with a book that you hate.

For young readers there are picture books with just a word or two, books of rhymes and jump rope chants, alphabet books, concept books (over, under, etc.), pattern stories, repeated readings, folk and fairy tales, wordless books providing an opportunity to create your own story, and many more.

You might also consider storytelling and retelling, singing songs, and book/tape combinations. Try making your own books with photographs from your adventures together, or have the child dictate to you, then do the drawings. As your child grows, let her make her own book using inventive spelling. (The child writes the word the way she thinks it sounds.) Create a personal dictionary by adding a word to a blank book, which has been divided alphabetically, each time you are asked how to spell a word. Get a beginning dictionary or encyclopedia and help your child look up the spelling or information she wants.

Purchase some easy-to-read books that can be tackled again and again. Check out longer picture books and short chapter books from the library. Take turns reading sentences, pages, or chapters, or each of you can take on the role of one of the characters. Explore unison reading. Encourage your child to read to siblings or younger friends.

Investigate comic books, jokes and riddles, magazines, fables and myths, poetry, information books, biographies, autobiographies, and historical fiction. Compare stories retold by different authors, or compare a novel to the movie or television counterpart. If you are looking for quality novels or picture books, the Caldecott and Newbery Award winners are a good place to start. Young Readers' Choice nominations give youngsters a chance to express their opinions about what they read. Your library has lists of award winning books, and may even shelve them together for your convenience.

As your child matures in reading skills, consider point of view stories, historical novels, classics, science fiction and biographies.

Children are naturally motivated to learn reading skills through games that require reading, scavenger hunts, recipes, experiment manuals, notes from Mom and Dad, pen pals, and restaurant menus. If there are words to be read, and your child has an interest, just about anything can be used to help a child learn to read.

Late Readers

Is your child slow to begin reading? Don't worry! That is easier said than done, particularly when a sibling, sometimes a younger sibling, or the public school child across the street is reading chapter books and your child hasn't mastered *One Fish, Two Fish*, and worse yet, doesn't appear to have any desire to read. Try to avoid panicking, calm yourself, and don't let your child know that you are worried. Sometimes it is helpful to find an adult who now enjoys reading who was also a late reader. It can give your child (and you) some perspective.

Many children do not learn to read until somewhere between ages ten and twelve. If your child is a late reader, be happy he is homeschooling and not in school being labeled learning disabled (because he is not) or feeling humiliated by teachers and peers. Reassure your child (if he is concerned) that he will find his own time and way of learning. Tell him over and over that you know he loves reading because he enjoys being read to. Remind him that everyone is unique.

One young friend went from struggling with *One Fish, Two Fish* to reading three or four chapter books a week in a matter of months. A nine year old acquaintance began to be interested in reading in March, and was reading at grade level by December. Late readers quickly catch up with peers, so they aren't handicapped for starting late. As a matter of fact, many late readers may have more interest in reading, once they learn, than some early readers. Be patient and have confidence in your child.

About Spelling

I haven't yet seen a spelling text that I love. A homemade alphabetized book in which children can record words which cause them trouble is the most useful spelling instruction tool I have used.

You and your child can watch for spelling patterns as you read and make up a rules for patterns if you wish. Work with other types of patterns is helpful also. Collect troublesome words from the child's written work to study. Play word games and invent codes; do crosswords, anagrams, and word hunts. The more you play with words, the better your spelling becomes.

The traditional method of studying a troublesome word incorporates several learning styles. Try this method and see if it works for your child:

Look at the word. Say the word. Close your eyes and imagine the word written on a chalkboard in your mind. Trace the word in the air with your hand. Open your eyes, and without looking at the word, write the word on your paper. Check the word. If an error is made, repeat the process.

Simple, huh? Works about as well as anything else. This method uses visual, auditory, and kinesthetic learning techniques, and requires no special materials or books. Practice of difficult words could be set to music; words could be spelled to the beat of a drum or metronome. Use your imagination to engage your child in learning to spell difficult words.

The biggest mistake parents and teachers can make with children who spell poorly is to require perfection. If demands for perfect spelling are made from an early age, the most likely result will be an adult with an aversion to both spelling and writing. Always allow the child to spell inventively on the first draft while he is getting his thoughts down on paper. Later, help him correct the spelling on *selected* first drafts during editing sessions. Help him learn to edit those letters to Grandma, stories for the newsletter, or a special poem. Edit for publication, but don't require him to edit everything he writes.

Be sure to keep some "spelling helpers" around the house, and help your child learn to use them. In addition to a good dictionary and a thesaurus, a number of tools are available that can help your child produce correctly spelled written work. There may be helpful spelling books to be found in the writing section of your bookstore. Some children may benefit from phonics study.

An electronic speller or a computer with a spell checker are both useful spelling tools. Spell checking software not only helps the poor speller produce a correctly spelled document, but it forces him to consider many possible spellings for a word and to make a choice. (One adult writer of poetry and fiction, a truly atrocious speller, admitted that his spelling actually improved after getting and using a spell checker.)

If a child continues to struggle with spelling as he matures, parents often become anxious. Try to relax. Whether or not he can spell well naturally or must always use tools to help him find and correct his own spelling mistakes is a secondary concern. Remember that the goal is to be able to find correct spellings when writing for others, not to win the spelling bee.

The secret of education lies in respecting the pupil.
—RALPH WALDO EMERSON

CHAPTER 7

A Sidelong Glance At The History Of Homeschooling

Did you know that the word "homeschool" found a place in a dictionary recently? Isn't that great? We have a brand new word to describe the learning activity that has taken place within families and communities from the beginning of civilization! Children have been learning in and with their families for all this time without a word to describe that activity. We can well ask, why did a need arise for such a word, now, in the late twentieth century?

Until one hundred fifty or so years ago, homeschooling, with no name at all, was the norm. Children learned how to survive and to make a living through life with their families and in the community. Mothers and fathers taught their children what they needed to know or established them in apprenticeships.

To be sure, children of well-to-do families attended private schools or had private tutors. In addition, many church groups assumed the responsibility for educating the children of their congregations. For many people, however, formal schooling was unaffordable, or otherwise unavailable. Children learned "adult" skills within their families or through apprenticeships.

Public schooling is actually "the new kid on the block." In the United States, Horace Mann and others developed the idea of public, compulsory, schooling by 1850.

The intent of the public school system was to mold the huge influx of immigrants, with all their ethnic, cultural, and language differences, into patriotic, English-speaking, factory workers and laborers. Available to all American children, the public schools gave many poor people a chance to learn to read, write, and figure, whether their parents had these skills or not. Public school seemed to offer a new opportunity and removed the burden of educating children from their parents.

It was not long, however, before public schooling and its bureaucratic ways began to interfere with actual learning. As public schools became more cumbersome, bureaucratic, and inflexible, families became disillusioned with their neighborhood schools. With disillusionment came a search for alternatives. Alternatives included traditional private schooling, alternative schools of every kind, and finally—homeschooling.

Alternative educators, notably John Holt, began to turn away from public schooling as well. Holt, as shown in his book *How Children Learn*, was an astute student of how children learn. He clearly saw the ways in which schooling interferes with children's learning. Holt saw that all children are gifted if allowed to grow and develop in a healthy, loving, enriching environment.

Holt opened the way for many "pioneer homeschoolers" to trust themselves and their children enough to leave schools and to discover the world for themselves. In 1977, Holt founded a newsletter, *Growing Without Schooling*, which still teems with stories of children growing, learning, and developing their intellectual and other gifts free from the rigors of schooling. Holt wrote many other books about children and learning, and addressed the homeschooling community in his classic *Teach Your Own*.

Another educator who is popular with many homeschoolers is Dr. Raymond Moore. Dr. Moore and his wife Dorothy have argued persuasively that children should not be subjected to early schooling. In *Better Late Than Early*, the Moores have focused on the harm that early reading and paper and pencil type activities can cause. In *Homeschool Burnout* they offer tips to families who struggle to adjust to the homeschooling lifestyle. The Moores have been most influential in the Christian homeschooling movement.

Fundamentalist Christians first increased public awareness of the homeschooling movement during the 80's. At that time large numbers of Christians peeled off from traditional private, parochial, and public schools and began to homeschool their children. These homeschoolers quickly organized, and began to generate legal changes in many states, including Oregon. Unfortunately, some of the new laws were narrowly focused and did not consider the diverse needs of the entire homeschooling community.

The general homeschooling population has continued to grow at a slow, steady rate. New laws in several states have been carefully drawn to allow for the diversity of style and method that characterizes homeschooling. Inclusive organizations, materials, and magazines are now available to meet the diverse needs of the homeschooling population. It appears that, for many people, homeschooling is not a bandwagon to jump on this week and off next week. Choosing homeschooling is a life-changing decision made after long and careful thought. The decision to homeschool may be the first step toward a more family-centered way of life.

What kind of people choose to become homeschooling families? There are probably as many types of homeschooling families as there are types of families and children. Homeschoolers are: urban, suburban, and rural; wealthy, middle-class, and poor; members of many races and ethnic backgrounds; two at-home parents, one at-home parent, both parents work, single-parent family; religious and nonreligious; to be found throughout the world; vary in size from one child to many children; public school drop-outs, private school rise-outs, unschoolers, non-schoolers, part-time schoolers; conservative and liberal; Republican and Democrat. Name any characteristic and you'll probably find some homeschoolers that fit the description.

What is the future of homeschooling? As far as anyone can tell, homeschooling is here to stay. Homeschooled children excel, both academically and socially. Homeschooled children develop strong value systems and personal interests. Homeschooled families demonstrate a high degree of social concern. Where else can you find such richly diverse families working side by side to guarantee each other the right to educate their own children? I don't know that answer, but I do know this: Homeschooling is good for what ails this country!

That so few now dare to be eccentric
marks the chief danger of the time.
—JOHN STUART MILL

CHAPTER 8

When People Criticize Your Decision To Homeschool . . .

Fewer than one percent of school-age children are presently homeschooled. Still far from society's norm, homeschooling raises eyebrows. Homeschooling parents can expect criticism and should be prepared to handle it.

How can a family present its choice to learn at home as a serious, carefully made decision, without inviting a barrage of criticism? When the decision to homeschool is under attack, how can we best use the moment to educate our critics? Can critics be turned into allies?

Three points should be considered to better enable you to speak effectively and respectfully when defending your decision to homeschool.

First, assume that the people who criticize really do have the best interests of your children at heart. Their personal education, however good or bad it may have been, is valuable to them, and they sincerely want your children to have as good an education as they had. Often they themselves don't feel qualified to teach their own children, and they project that perceived lack onto other families. Critics wonder whether you are qualified to teach your children. They may be afraid that the children will suffer irreparable harm. Another source of criticism is professional teachers, who find everything they believe in, their very means of livelihood, even their purpose for being, threatened by home education. These concerned individuals must be taken very seriously.

Second, your decision to educate your children at home may be considered a judgment call against other peoples' decisions to send their children to a public school. You may be thought of as a snob, an elitist. Your act of choice may be interpreted as abandonment of public schools. People who criticize homeschooling may feel they must defend their personal beliefs about education and schooling. They must even consider whether school in general is a good thing.

Third, and very significant, almost everyone in our culture sees "education" and "schooling" as the same. Thus, your decision to keep your children out of school may be viewed, consciously or otherwise, as a decision to deprive your children of "education." Homeschoolers have the added responsibility to educate the community that homeschooling is an acceptable alternative to public or private schooling.

With these points in mind, the following tips may be useful when speaking with those who criticize homeschooling.

- You have a philosophy of learning that is uniquely yours. Share it! The decision to homeschool is a major, life-altering decision. Let people know that you know what you are doing. Help them realize that you did not arrive at your decision to homeschool lightly. You did not choose to keep your kids out of school because you are still mad at your fifth grade teacher or because Susie pulled Billy's hair once too often. You have thought long and hard about it and are ready to talk about your reasons for homeschooling with interested people.

- Let people know that, while anyone CAN homeschool, not everyone will or should choose to homeschool. When people hear you say that, they know you are not trying to convert them. You just want them to know that you know what you are doing. Homeschooling takes a significant commitment of time and energy. Not everyone can make that kind of commitment, and they should not be made to feel guilty. One candid mother, upon hearing me talk about my homeschooling experiences, told me, "It sounds like a good idea, but I couldn't do it. I like to shop too much."

- Save your worries, fears, and complaints about homeschooling for support group meetings. Let's face it, homeschooling can be work. Drawbacks, such as lack of privacy, housework never caught up, and constant driving, can cause frustration for families as they begin to develop a homeschooling lifestyle. Most critics of homeschooling will consider your complaints to be a sign that homeschooling does not work. Their fears that you may ruin your children seem to be validated when you complain. Your casual complaint about a minor frustration may invite an extra measure of criticism.

- Actively present a positive image in the community. You don't have to go on television or be constantly in public to show the world how great homeschooling is for your family. When shopping with the kids at 10 o'clock Monday morning, chat with the clerks about today's cooking project, or field trip, or whatever, before they even get a chance to ask why the kids aren't in school today. If they do ask, you can answer, "My children learn at home, and we have a flexible schedule."

  Devise comments that tell strangers that, not only is homeschooling an acceptable way to learn, but a highly desirable one for your family! Don't forget to tell them how glad you are that their children are doing so well in public school! Such positive presentations create a buffer zone around you. People may still be highly critical of homeschooling, but they may also be less likely to confront you negatively.

- Speak of what you want for your children, not what you are avoiding. Almost everyone can agree that one-on-one instruction is ideal. Don't complain that public classrooms are too crowded and the children waste their time while compelled to be there — just a tad negative, right? You can praise the advantages of one-on-one instruction without condemning anyone else's choices.

  Home learning offers individual attention to children's interests and developmental patterns. I can tell my friends that my children already knew how to do first grade math, or to read, and I did not want to interrupt their learning pattern. If the children are late starters, I can say that I did not want the children to start school until they were ready for the rigors of formal schooling.

Rather than judging the merits of a neighborhood school, or schooling in general, I merely affirm that I have taken charge of my children's education.

•   Learn to use "Ed Speak." You remember those comments on the back of report cards? "Mary respects the rights of others" means that Mary does not steal from, hit, kick, or yell at the other kids. "Ed Speak" is jargon for common, ordinary events. It is used effectively to snow "outsiders."

Take fractions, for example. Did the little kids play with the measuring cups while the big kids made a double batch of chocolate chip cookies? No, no. They studied math using manipulatives in practical life activities. Even more to the obscure point, the little kids learned about volume and capacity of dissimilar containers. The older kids did an experiment that exposed them to some basic principles of math, physics, and chemistry. They also reviewed the multiplication of fractions.

Did your four year old ask questions until you turned blue? He developed exhaustive questioning strategies (really!). Who wrote out the shopping list? That person worked on spelling and handwriting. Did the eight year old write "Keep Out!" signs and post them on her bedroom door? Creative writing! Did your daughter call you Benedict Arnold when you did not keep a promise? Your history lessons have not been wasted! She has internalized her knowledge.

You can have some fun playing around with "Ed Speak." The basic rule is to use obscure, vague, and polysyllabic (see?) words to cast specific actions into broad categories.

•   Speak occasionally of the personal rewards you gain from homeschooling your children. "I homeschool my children because I love to spend time with them." "I have always wanted to study science, and here is my chance!" Such comments generate, if not acceptance, or even envy, at least some sense of, "Oh, well, to each his own."

- Make it your business to develop a positive reputation for the work you are doing homeschooling your kids. If your kids are polite, friendly, have good playing habits, and a strong measure of self esteem, their actions speak more strongly for homeschooling than any words you can ever say. My parents were not sure I was doing a good thing by homeschooling my young children. After many years of watching the growth and development of my sister's homeschooled children and my own, my parents now defend homeschooling in their community. Why? Because they have seen the results, and the results are good.

- Invite neighborhood schoolchildren into your home after school and in the summertime. Include them from time to time in some of your activities. Neighborhood parents will quickly learn that your kids are doing okay. You might even find potential critics coming to you to find out what homeschoolers do all day long. More than one neighbor child has confided in me that their moms said they would homeschool too, if they could.

- Be prepared to field the "Socialization Question." The socialization question is often just this: "What about socialization?" It can be fun and effective to say, simply, "Yes, isn't it great that we can avoid the negative socializing situations in schools?"

  Many of our critics, however, believe that the positive aspects of school socialization outweigh the negative aspects. Rather than succumb to the temptation to argue that point, it is easier to show how readily positive socialization opportunities are found in the community. Share a little bit about your children's friendships, their group activities through church, community, homeschool groups, scouts, 4-H, etc. Reassure concerned individuals that you have given the socialization issue some thought, too, and are making sure your children connect with the outside world.

  Recently I responded to a store clerk's concern: "But what about socialization?" I simply said, "I agree with you, the socialization issue is very important. Homeschoolers are very concerned about socializing their children. Participation in community and homeschooling groups gives the children many opportunities to make friends and to learn how to work in a group. It isn't always easy, but they soon learn how to meet strangers and to find their own friends."

With some people it can be helpful to address specific socialization questions, such as: How does she play? Does she have the skills to find and keep friends on her own when she reaches adulthood? Can she resolve differences with friends by using words and compromise? Can she stand up for her beliefs and values? Does she know how to spend time alone? Does she have effective and appropriate ways of handling emotions? Does she have both leading and following skills? Is forced membership in large, age-segregated groups the only way to teach social skills?

- Above all, be respectful of your critic's right to have opinions that are different from yours. Isn't that what we want for ourselves? Homeschoolers want the right to choose their own way, without being judged, condemned, or discriminated against. Homeschooling parents want the freedom to make educational choices for their children, and they are willing to take responsibility for those decisions. Those who criticize homeschooling deserve no less.

CHAPTER 9

Finding Apprenticeships

An apprenticeship can be a valuable experience for the older homeschool student. Older youngsters are ready to join the real world, accept real responsibility, tackle real challenges, and meet real people. A good apprenticeship provides such opportunities.

Your child's interests are the best starting point. Perhaps she enjoys bicycling and is mechanically inclined. Ask at some bicycle shops for opportunities there. Perhaps he enjoys drawing. Contact a local graphic artist's association for possible leads for a professional artist who might be willing to have an apprentice. The possibilities are as varied as your imagination and your willingness to put yourself and your child out there. Don't be afraid of a "no." Keep searching until you find a fit.

Look for connections in your neighborhood and with friends, relatives, and business associates. It may only be a matter of keeping your eyes and ears open. Perhaps the retired person down the street is an accomplished gardener and would enjoy the company of a young person. He would gain an opportunity to share his abundant knowledge and the help of an extra pair of hands. Perhaps you have a friend who is a gourmet cook and needs help with her weekly dinner parties. Maybe an uncle would welcome a young plumber as a helper.

Don't forget to consider opportunities to do community service. These opportunities also can provide valuable real life experiences. Community service tasks are real work and can be a springboard to additional opportunities.

Apprenticeships can last for a week, can happen once a week for a month, or may be several hours a day for a year. Your child might experience one apprenticeship a year or many.

It is important for parents to get involved in helping set up apprenticeships. The adult expert will feel more comfortable and you will provide a good model for your homeschool student. Do remember to give your youngster an opportunity to talk with the potential mentor as well, so each has an opportunity to decide whether this might be a workable arrangement. Also be sure to follow-up on how things are going regularly with both your child and her mentor, so you can help iron out any difficulties.

As your youngster matures and is ready to venture away from home, he or she may want to consider ideas similar to these apprenticeships that others have tried: conservation work in Australia; apprenticing to be a master farmer in Greece; interning in a museum in Micronesia; working with a midwife in Kentucky; volunteering with disabled children in England; studying art in Italy; working as a teacher or doing construction in India; helping a team of solid-state physics researchers in Holland; or interning as a wildlife patient care assistant in New York.

An apprenticeship doesn't have to be far from home in order to be successful, though. For some young people, traveling and being away from home is part of their learning. Others can achieve the goals they desire simply by finding meaningful involvement in work they love in their own communities and neighborhoods.

Once she has experienced "small" apprenticeships close to home, your child may be equipped with the skills to go out and find such an adventure. If you need help, there are several helpful organizations listed in Chapter 14. You might advertise in state and national homeschooling newsletters for the kinds of opportunities you seek.

Part Two

How-To-
Homeschool
Resources

You cannot teach a man anything;
you can only help him find it within himself.
—GALILEO

CHAPTER 10
Homeschooling Periodicals

First things first! Start reading about homeschooling now and read as much as you possibly can. Schools call it professional development or teacher training. It is just plain good sense to learn as much as you can about how children learn and how to teach your children. Reading from the growing body of work on homeschooling can go a long way towards building confidence that you, too, can successfully homeschool your children.

It is essential that homeschoolers subscribe to at least one of the following national periodicals, in addition to state and local newsletters. Think of it! Every two months or so, just as your homeschooling spirits are beginning to sag, a panel of experienced, successful homeschoolers arrives via your mailbox and engages you in discussions of the very same homeschooling questions that were troubling you, right there in the privacy of your home. Who could ask for more?

If subscription cost is a problem, encourage your local library to subscribe to your favorites. Or you might form a "magazine cooperative" with several homeschooling friends, and share subscriptions.

Several highly recommended, well-known national magazines are reviewed below, to give you an idea of the differences among them.

Several offer a Christian perspective, including one from a fundamentalist Christian perspective. Some espouse a structured school-at-home method; others encourage unschooling, or something between the two extremes.

I have chosen to review these major magazines here, together, for several reasons. First, the general homeschooling movement and the fundamentalist Christian movement are inextricably entwined. From time to time, we need to work together, and it helps to know what is going on in the "other" camp. To do so it is important for people from many philosophical positions to understand as much as possible about the other points of view.

Several other periodicals with unique approaches or audiences are listed in the National Resources and Periodicals section in Chapter 12 and may be preferred by some homeschoolers.

While we may disagree sharply on how to teach reading, we probably all agree that families have the right to choose the method of teaching reading for their families. What you will find is that, in spite of sharp differences in style, method, and philosophy, homeschooling families have much more in common than most people think. Don't we all want to direct the content and method of our children's instruction? Don't we all want a great education for our children? Don't we all want to preserve our right to homeschool?

If, after reading the reviews, you are still unsure which magazines best fit your homeschooling style, order a sample copy of each and see for yourself. (I enjoy receiving them all when I can afford it — what can I say?)

❖

Growing Without Schooling (GWS)
Published by Pat Farenga. Holt Associates, 2269 Mass. Ave.,
Cambridge MA 02140. Six annual 32 page issues, $25 per year. Single
issue costs $4.50. An index for issues 1 - 85 is available for $5.95.

GWS was founded in 1977 by John Holt, who is one of the
important thinkers of our time on how people learn. Holt started the
newsletter after he became convinced that public schools were not
going to respond to what he had been saying for years about how
children learn and what causes them to fail. When a few daring people
began to take their children out of school and teach them at home, Holt
turned his attention away from trying to help schools improve. Instead,
he began to assist these early homeschooling families. GWS continues
to espouse unschooling in reflection of Holt's philosophy. However,
homeschoolers with many different educational philosophies are given
support, help and encouragement in this newsletter.

The bulk of the writing in GWS is in the form of personal
accounts of individual families' homeschooling experiences, excerpted
from letters that homeschooling readers (both parents and children)
have written to GWS. This newsletter is a support group by mail,
reassuring readers that they too can homeschool. GWS has served as a
sole source of support for many homeschoolers for years.

Some issues of the newsletter have a theme, with a number of
letters addressing a particular topic. Recently editor Susannah Sheffer
has sent out search letters to homeschooling children, asking them to
address specific issues such as socialization, or handling boredom, and
including excerpts from the students' replies in the Focus feature.

Other features include national news and reports, a
homeschooling events calendar, pen pals, declassified ads, display
advertising, and listings of resource people and recommendations,
including helpful teachers, school districts, special interests and needs,
and others. There are usually a few book reviews in each issue, and an
update on new materials available at *John Holt's Book and Music
Store*.

A directory of subscribers who wish to be listed is published
annually, with updates and additions listed in each issue. The Directory
has been instrumental in helping homeschoolers find each other.

Besides carrying the learning legacy of John Holt to
homeschooling families, GWS provides a good forum for individual
homeschoolers to address issues of concern. It is an excellent source of
support and information.

❖

Home Education Magazine (HEM)
Published by Mark and Helen Hegener, Home Education Press, PO
Box 1083, Tonasket WA 98855. (509)486-1351. Bi-monthly 68 page
issues, $24 per year, with discounts offered. Single issue, $4.50. Back
issues and booklet reprints of articles of special interests are available.

HEM was founded by Mark and Helen Hegener in 1983.
Home Education Magazine has become a well-known national,
inclusive, homeschooling magazine. The editors courageously discuss
and clarify "sticky" homeschool issues, and seek the cutting edge of
homeschooling concerns.

HEM accepts all styles of homeschooling without judgment,
and the editorial position focuses on the individual freedom and
personal responsibility that can be attained through home education.

HEM features articles and columns written by well-known
and well-respected homeschoolers, including Kaseman, Rupp, Dobson,
and Creech. Each issue includes articles on one or more different
themes that address timely homeschooling topics. Useful tips, ideas,
and resources for both new and veteran homeschooling families can be
found in every issue.

One feature is "Newswatch," which informs homeschooling
families about local and national coverage of home education. This
feature offers an opportunity to stay apprised of any national trend that
might develop that could affect homeschooling. Another popular
feature is "Good Stuff," resource reviews by Rebecca Rupp. You can
find out what the favorite homeschooling resources are and why. The
most recent feature, "Software Review," promises to bring valuable
information to families who use computers in their homeschooling
activities.

Letters from readers are welcomed and encouraged, resource
materials are reviewed, and a pen pal section is offered. Other features
include the Homeschool Notebook, a listing of Support Groups and
Organizations by state, unclassifieds, resource addresses, an advertisers
index, and regular columnists.

In the past, HEM has been the first national homeschooling
magazine to address key issues that have impacted all homeschoolers
of all philosophies across the country. As far as I can tell, HEM
continues to lead the way in keen analysis of popular educational
thinking, both within and outside of the homeschooling community.

Some of the best and most thoughtful writing about
homeschooling can be found in *Home Education Magazine*.

❖

The Moore Report International (MRI)
Published by The Moore Foundation, Box 1, Camas WA 98607,
(206)835-2736. Bi-monthly 16 page tabloid, $12 per year.

MRI is published by The Moore Foundation, "which primarily
serves educators in public, private, and home schools. It is not a
policy-making body. It imposes no stand on religion, politics, nor
methods on its clients or supporters. It does not compete with state
support groups, but offers service to anyone requesting assistance."
(Please note that the Moores and the Moore Foundation separated from
the Hewitt Foundation in 1988.)

Raymond and Dorothy Moore are the pioneers of the
Christian homeschooling movement. Dr. Raymond Moore has long
been an educator and education researcher, and advocated for delayed
schooling at about the same time (1950's and 1960's) that John Holt
was advocating for general school reform. The "Moore homeschooling
formula," a balance of study, entrepreneurship, and service, has helped
many homeschooling families to avoid the burnout caused by too much
book work. Except for advocating the controversial practices of
scheduling babies and disciplining through spanking (rare use only),
the Moore philosophy is generally respectful of children's natural ways
of learning.

Each issue contains editorials by both Dorothy and Raymond
Moore, as well as other homeschooling writers, including Dr. Ruth
Beechick. *The Moore Report International* focuses on local, regional,
national and international home education news. It usually includes
articles on legal and legislative issues, research, and other general
education news. Also included are display advertising, letters to the
editor, Curriculum Kernels, questions and answers, and noteworthy
quotes. The rift between some fundamentalist Christian homeschooling
families and the rest of the homeschooling movement is of great
concern to the Moores, and contrary to their philosophy of acceptance.

Order forms and description lists for the Moore Foundation
Curriculum Programs, learning materials, and books are available in
each issue. A complete listing of Moore conferences and seminars is
also included.

If you want to know what the Moores are thinking and doing,
what worries them, and what encourages them in the homeschooling
world as well as other educational arenas, subscribe now.

❖

Practical Homeschooling (PH)
Published by Mary Pride, Home Life, PO Box 1250, Fenton MO
63026-1850. Editorial Fax: (314)225-0743. E-mail at
marypride@aol.com. Four issues per year, 80 pages, $15, or $25 for
eight issues. Back issues available at $5.

Practical Homeschooling is a relatively new, glossy, full-color
magazine in the homeschooling market, but publisher Mary Pride has
been on the homeschooling scene for years. *The Big Book of Home
Learning* and *Pride's Guide to Educational Software,* Mary's
collections of reviews of curriculum, educational products, and
educational software, have helped many homeschooling families find
the resources they want.

This magazine should be subtitled " . . . for Christian
homeschoolers and their friends." While *PH* presents itself as
inclusive(at least, no editorial policy states otherwise), articles,
opinions, and advertising are predominantly from a Christian
perspective.

PH intends to fill perceived gaps that other homeschooling
magazines, books, and seminars may miss. Included in every issue will
be: coverage of a variety of homeschooling methods, including unit
studies, Charlotte Mason, accelerated education, and on-line education;
elementary and preschool education; high school and college helps;
high tech education; many reviews, time and money saving tips,
personal stories and more. *PH* carries a great deal of advertising, both
secular and Christian, and includes an advertisers index. All is
seasoned with Mary's personality and sense of fun.

PH is less focused on the political aspect of homeschooling
and more focused on the practical apects. Columns are written by
popular Christian homeschool writers, including Duffy, Andreola,
Blumenfeld, Hulcy, Swan, Somerville, and others. Articles are practical
and timely, offering useful tips, and are based on current research and
educational thinking.

People who enjoy Mary Pride's perspective should definitely
try this magazine. If you are a Christian homeschooling family looking
for a moderate perspective, this magazine may meet your needs
perfectly.

❖

The Teaching Home: A Christian Magazine for Home Educators (TTH)
Published by Sue Welch, PO Box 20219, Portland OR 97220-0219, (503)253-9633. 64 to 88 pages, $15 per year. Back issues are available at $3.75 each or less. Sample copy $3.75.

The Teaching Home has evolved from its 1981 beginnings as a five page Portland area newsletter for the Christian Home Education Association (now OCEAN), into a glossy, traditional style national magazine that reaches thousands of Christian homeschoolers today.

TTH's stated purpose is "to provide information, inspiration, and support to Christian home-schooled families and organizations." Further, it states that "the organization, and all of its activities and publications, will be consistently and forthrightly Christian to the honor and glory of the Lord God." Many articles are liberally sprinkled with Biblical quotes, references, and prayer.

The writing and advertising in *The Teaching Home* supports the "church school at home" model of homeschooling. A Special Section in each issue focuses on a particular homeschooling topic of interest. Regular features cover convention and workshop news, legal news, teaching tips, samplings of Christian newsletters from around the country, letters to the editor, a short humor section, and an editorial by Michael Farris, President of Home School Legal Defense Association. The cover story of each issue spotlights a Christian homeschooling family. *The Oregon Update* is a supplemental section that provides state-specific information, listing only fundamentalist events, and addressing legal and legislative concerns from a fundamentalist Christian perspective.

The magazine carries extensive display advertising for Christian materials (more than twenty full pages in a recent issue) and is very selective in accepting advertisements. An Advertisers' Index is included.

If you are looking for homeschooling guidance and pre-screened materials from the fundamentalist Christian point of view, look no further.

❖

Homeschooling Today: Practical help for Christian Families
Published by S Squared Productions, PO Box 1425, Melrose FL 32666.
Sixty-eight pages. Subscription is $20 per year for six issues.

This magazine is another newcomer on the scene, and looks promising. It focuses on giving practical tips and lessons that you can do right now. Many regular features include Unit Studies, Living Literature, Preschool Activities, Science Corner, Working With Teens, and Product Review.

One especially nice feature is the pull-out art lesson, which includes a full color reproduction of a work of art along with teaching suggestions, activities, and information about both the work and the artist.

There is plenty of advertising, and there is an Advertisers Index. Products are not prescreened, but the magazine may limit advertisements within a broad spectrum of Christian standards.

If you enjoy unit studies with a Christian perspective, you will find reading this magazine very helpful.

CHAPTER 11

Books To Get You Started And Keep You Going

Homeschooling Books

These books deal specifically with homeschooling issues: how to do it, people's homeschooling stories, general resources, political issues, etc. Books without listed publishers can usually be found in your local library, through inter-library loan, or try John Holt's Book Store, Home Education Press, or Out of the Box Publishing (Addresses are given at the end of this listing). My favorites are marked with R.

Better Than School: One Family's Declaration of Independence, by Nancy Wallace. A personal book about one family's experience. The author tells the story of life with a difficult school board. Nancy also wrote *Child's Work*, about how Nancy's children grew and, in the course of pursuing their interests, developed talents in music, writing, art, and other subject areas, learning their biggest lessons as they played. **R**

The Big Book of Home Learning, by Mary Pride. 1987, 1988. If you are still not sure what materials you want for your children, try this book. The author has a strong Christian perspective, is highly opinionated, and reviews many secular and Christian educational materials from many sources. This book has been republished as a four volume set. The set is expensive, but it might be a useful addition to your neighborhood library if they don't already have it.

Family Learning Cooperatives, by Jane A. Williams. 1992. Bluestocking Press, PO Box 1014, Placerville CA 95667-1014. Provides a useful model for developing learning cooperatives for older homeschoolers, based on the Sudbury Valley school, and other models. Sample contracts, agreements, and questionnaires are included. It seems to have everything you might need to start a learning co-op.

Family Matters: Why Homeschooling Makes Sense, by David Guterson, available from Home Education Press. A thought-provoking discussion. This homeschooling dad and high school English teacher makes his case for homeschooling and addresses many of the issues that are of concern to all parents. **R**

The First Home-School Catalogue, 2nd edition, by Donn Reed. 1986. An alphabetical guide to many items, sources of material, information, and names of support groups.

For New Homeschoolers. 1992. Published by Home Education Press. $2.00. A booklet of articles to help get you started, addressing common concerns about homeschooling, including tips for low-cost homeschooling. **R**

Good Stuff: Learning Tools for All Ages, by Rebecca Rupp. Home Education Press, 1993, $14.75. A wide-ranging resource book that is full of resources for programs, supplies, music, games, workbooks, videos, toys, computer programs, catalogs, periodicals and fiction and nonfiction books for various grade levels. Several indexes for easy reference. **R**

Hard Times In Paradise, by David and Micki Colfax. Published by Mountain House Press, PO Box 353, Philo CA 94566. $19.95. A story of the many difficulties and challenges the Colfaxes experienced on their "forty-seven acre classroom," and how three of their boys were admitted to Harvard. **R**

Home and School Reading and Study Guides. 1989. A Grolier supplement to *The New Book of Knowledge.*

Home Education and Constitutional Liberties, by John Whitehead and Wendell Bird. 1986. Crossway Books, Westchester IL. Discusses many basic constitutional liberties that support your right to educate your children yourself.

Home School Burnout, by Raymond and Dorothy Moore. The Moore Foundation, PO Box 1, Camas WA 98607. If you are certain that you want a structured, scheduled homeschool, this book offers guidance. Too much structure can lead to burnout, and the Moores offer a formula to balance family life and structured academics.

The Home School Manual: For Parents Who Teach Their Own Children, by Theodore E. Wade, Jr., 1988, 1994. Gazelle Publications, 5580 Stanley Drive, Auburn CA 95603. Structured, school-at-home, parent-as-teacher approach. Christian emphasis, but attempts to be inclusive. The fifth revision is just out.

The Home School Reader, edited by Mark and Helen Hegener. Home Education Press. Intelligent, humorous, well-written articles by some of the best homeschooling writers across the country. Issues such as socialization, accountability, teaching reading, discipline, handling freedom, selecting curricular materials, and much more. Currently being revised. **R**

The Home School Resource Book, by Donn Reed. Brook Farm Books, PO Box 246, Bridgewater ME 04735. Combines two titles into one volume: *The First Home-School Catalog* and *The Home-School Challenge*. Reviews books and learning materials with comments and essays.

Home School: Taking the First Step, by Borg Hendrickson. 1989. Mountain Meadow Press, PO Box 447, Kooskia ID 83539. A how-to teaching guide with planning and teaching tips and resources. Written by a teacher.

Home Schools: An Alternative, You Do Have a Choice! by Cheryl Gorder. 1987. Manual for decision making and guidance, includes resources. Answers many common questions.

Home-Based Education in the United States: An Annotated Bibliography, by Sandra Hendrickson. 1988.

Homeschooling and the Public Schools. 1992 reprint from *Home Education Magazine*, $2.00 postpaid. Covers a wide range of topics related to the public schools.

Homeschooling and Research. 1992 reprint from *Home Education Magazine*, $2.00 postpaid. Explores the many questions surrounding research and homeschooling. Homeschoolers are often asked to participate in research. Read this booklet before you decide to participate in research.

*Homeschooling Freedoms at Ris*k, reprinted from *Home Education Magazine*, $2.00 postpaid. While this booklet is not essential to the beginning homeschooler, it is important reading. It addresses the problems that arise when one group of homeschoolers claims to represent the needs and best interests of all homeschoolers. If your homeschooling group claims to have all the information you will ever need to be able to homeschool, read this pamphlet. Essential reading for support group leaders. **R**

*Homeschooling for Excellenc*e, by David and Micki Colfax. Mountain House Press, Box 353, Philo CA 95466, 1987. Experience of a northern California family well known for their homeschooled children who have attended Harvard. **R**

Homeschooling in the News, edited by Pat Farenga. John Holt's Book Store, $6.95. Contains reprints of articles about homeschooling from national newspapers and magazines, covering the years 1986 through January 1991.

*How to Begin Homeschooling: A Parent's Guid*e, by Judy Garvey. 1989. Gentle Wind School, PO Box 184, Surry ME 04684. $3.50, or free, if the cost is a hardship to you. A booklet for families who are considering removing their children from schools. **R**

*How to Stock a Quality Home Library Inexpensivel*y, by Jane Williams. Bluestocking Press, PO Box 1014, Placerville CA 95667-1014. A helpful guide for finding books.

How to Write a Low-Cost/No-Cost Curriculum for Your Home-School Child, by Borg Hendrickson. 1993. Mountain Meadow Press, PO Box 447, Kooskia ID 83539. A guide to developing your own traditional type curriculum to meet your child's needs. Being revised.

I Learn Better By Teaching Myself, by Agnes Leistico. Home Education Press. This book relates the story of one parent who changed from being a believer in traditional schooling to being an advocate for interest-initiated learning. R

In Their Own Way, by Thomas Armstrong. A popular book on teaching and learning that describes seven different personal learning styles, and ways that parents can encourage learning.

Letters Home, by Britt Barker. Home Education Press. A teenaged homeschooler writes about her learning and her travels around the world.

Learning All the Time, by John Holt. Emphasizes Holt's philosophy that children will teach themselves what they want and need to know.R

My Life as a Traveling Homeschooler, by Jennifer Goldman. Solomon Press Publishers, 417 Roslyn Road, Roslyn Heights NY 11577. Jennifer relates her experiences as a homeschooler as she travels with her uncle, alternative educator Jerry Mintz.

Playful Learning, by Anne Engelhart and Cheryl Sullivan. Can be obtained from your local La Leche League Group or from LLLI, PO Box 1209, Franklin Park IL 60131-8209, $14.95. Creative ideas for fun and learning at home for very young children. Excellent starting place for families who begin homeschooling in early childhood. R

Pride's Guide to Educational Software, by Bill and Mary Pride. Home Life, PO Box 1250, Fenton MO 63026-1850. More than 750 programs for DOS, Windows, MPC, Macintosh, Apple II family, and Amiga. Also CD-ROMs and videodiscs. Ask your librarian for it.

Real Lives: eleven teenagers who don't go to school, edited by Grace Llewellyn. Lowry House Publishers, PO Box 1014, Eugene OR 97440-1014. Contains comprehensive essays written by unschooled teens from all over the country. Their homeschooling lives and interests are the basis for compelling stories of how these teens are educating themselves.

Schooling At Home, edited by Anne Pederson and Peggy O'Mara, 1990. Mothering, PO Box 1690, Santa Fe NM 87504, (505)984-8116, FAX (505)986-8335. Explores philosophies of learning, legal issues, methods of teaching, personal accounts of homeschooling.

Should I Teach My Kids at Home? by Kate Kerman. John Holt's Book and Music Store, $5.00. A useful workbook for parents.

Taking Charge Through Homeschooling: Personal and Political Empowerment, by Larry and Susan Kaseman. Koshkonong Press, 2545 Koshkonong Rd., Stoughton WI 53589. Guide to the role we can play in helping people identify their principles and beliefs. **R**

Teach Your Own, by John Holt. John Holt's Book and Music Store. Published in 1981, this book is the homeschooling classic, by the "guru" of unschooling. A must read for every homeschooling parent. Also by Holt: *Learning All The Time, Shared Treasures* (book reviews of homeschooling resources), *How Children Fail, How Children Learn, Freedom and Beyond, Instead of Education*, others. **R**

*The Teenage Liberation Handbook: how to get out of school and get a real life and educatio*n, by Grace Llewellyn. Lowry House Publishers, PO Box 1014, Eugene OR 97440. A resource book packed with information for teens who wish to leave school to begin learning on their own. **R**

*The Three R's at Hom*e, by Susan and Howard Richman. PA Homeschoolers, RD 2, Box 117, Kittanning PA 16201. One family's homeschooling story.

Typical Courses of Study, Kindergarten through Grade 12. World Book Educational Products, 101 Northwest Point Blvd., Elk Grove Village IL 60007. Nominal fee. An overview of courses typically used in schools. A useful guide for the home educator who wants to avoid expensive curricular materials. **R**

Write Your Own Curriculum: A Complete Guide to Planning, Organizing and Documenting Homeschool Curriculums, by Jenifer O'Leary. Whole Life Publishing Co., PO Box 936, Stevens Point WI 54481-0936. $12.95. Practical ideas for assessing individual needs, deciding what to study, keeping records, and staying organized. **R**

You Can Teach Your Child Successfully, The Three R's, by Ruth Beechick. Education Services, 6410 Raleigh Street, Arvada CO 80063. Details on what to teach in grades four through eight. Covers basic subjects plus Bible.

❖

Related Books

These books on related educational and family topics, while not specifically about homeschooling, provide an important backdrop for anyone who is concerned about education in America, including homeschooling parents. If you want to go beyond the basics of how to successfully homeschool your children, start here.

A Life Worth Living: Selected Letters of John Holt, edited by Susannah Sheffer, John Holt Book and Music Store. Learn more about the life and times of John Holt, the thinker. These letters are a fascinating study of the development of Holt's thinking from before his years of school teaching through his final years as a musician and homeschooling advocate. **R**

Alternatives in Education, by Mark and Helen Hegener. Home Education Press, revised 1992. Reviews the history and key elements of many education trends, including alternative education, homeschooling, Waldorf, Montessori, and much more. **R**

Goals 2000, An Education Strategy, US Department of Education, Washington DC, 20202-0498; (800)872-5327. Free, followed by frequent update newsletters. The source book for the long-range education plan to move every community in America toward the national education goals adopted by the president and the governors in 1991. Oregon's Katz bill, including Certificates of Mastery and outcome-based education, originated here.

Bringing Out the Best; A Resource Guide for Parents of Young Gifted Children, by Jacquelyn Saunders.

The Continuum Concept, by Jean Liedloff. Good background reading for those who view learning as a lifelong continuum.

Deschooling Society, by Ivan Illich. A classic which preceded the homeschooling trend by many years. Many of John Holt's ideas originated in conversations with Illich.

Dumbing Us Down: The Hidden Curriculum of Compulsory Schooling, by John Taylor Gatto. New Society Publishers, Philadelphia PA. Hard hitting essays include: *We Need Less School, Not More*; *The Seven-Lesson Schoolteacher; The Psychopathic School*; and others. After 26 years of award winning teaching in Manhattan, Gatto has quit teaching and has become an advocate for homeschooling and the radical reform of state schooling. **R**

Everyone is Able; Exploring the Myth of Learning Disabilities, by Susannah Sheffer, John Holt's Book and Music Store. True stories with helpful options.

The Exhausted School, by John Taylor Gatto. New Society Publishers, Philadelphia PA, 1992, or from John Holt's Book and Music Store. The account of the Carnegie Hall event, in which representatives of successful public, private, alternative, home, and self education programs and experiences shared their stories, and Gatto made a case for abandoning the models of education that do not work.

For Your Own Good: Hidden Cruelty in Child-Rearing and the Roots of Violence, by Alice Miller. Discusses the harm that can result for both the child and society when children are treated as less than equal.

Great Education Moves and *Rebound*. Radical, anonymous commentary about the desperate state of education in this country, with hope for homeschooling as a solution. Gentle Wind School, PO Box 184, Surry ME 04684.

How Children Learn, by John Holt. Holt's first book that describes his observations of children's learning processes, and how teachers and schools often interfere. **R**

How to Talk So Kids Will Listen & Listen So Kids Will Talk, by Adele Faber and Elaine Mazlish. Excellent practical discipline advice in an easy to read format. Learn how to avoid unnecessary parent/child conflict. **R**

Human Brain, Human Learning, by Leslie Hart. Discusses the brain, theories of how it works, and applies that knowledge to how children learn. An excellent read for scientific reassurance that experiential learning works.

Learning Denied, by Denny Taylor. Story of a capable child who was labeled Learning Disabled by school officials.

The Learning Mystique, by Gerald Coles, Ph. D.Challenges the idea that learning disabilities have a neurological basis, and proposes that we look instead at interactions. Good resource for challenging an LD diagnosis.

The Magic Feather, by Lori and Bill Granger. The truth about "special education." If your child has been negatively labeled, read this book.R

The Magical Child, by Joseph Chilton Pearce. "Rediscovering Nature's plan for our children."

The Myth of Learning Disabilities, edited by Susannah Sheffer. John Holt's Book and Music Store.

*None of the Above, Behind the Myth of Scholastic Aptitud*e, by David Owen. "How the Educational Testing Service controls the gates to higher education and success in American Society."

*Selling to the Other Educational Markets, 1993 Editio*n, by Jane A. Williams, Bluestocking Press, PO Box 1014, Placerville CA 95667. If you have an educational product to sell to homeschoolers, you may need this directory!

Siblings Without Rivalry, by Adele Faber & Elaine Mazlish. Companion book to *How to Talk So Kids Will Listen...* Excellent resource to help children learn to communicate effectively.

What Do You Really Want for Your Children? by Wayne Dyer. A book that helps parents help their youngsters to realize their full potential.

*Your Child's Growing Mind; A Parent's Guide to Learning from Birth to Adolescenc*e, by Jane M. Healy. Based on research in brain development, offers suggestions for how parents can provide a better environment for learning.

Your Child's Self-Esteem, by Dorothy Corkville Briggs. A good parenting book from birth to teens.

❖

How To Find Homeschooling Books

Try your public library, favorite local book merchant, or the mail order sources listed below.

- **Public Library:** In the Dewey Decimal System, homeschooling books are in Domestic Education, call number 649.68, home-based education, and also in Education, call numbers 371 and 372. They are classified LC 37 or LC 40 in the Library of Congress System. Check with the Children's Librarian to find out if a notebook of homeschooling resources is maintained.

- **Home Education Press**, PO Box 1083, Tonasket WA 98855 (509)486-1351

- **John Holt's Book and Music Store**, 2269 Mass.Ave., Cambridge MA 02140 (617)864-3100

- **Out of the Box Publishing**, PO Box 80214-B, Portland OR 97280. Selected favorites.

CHAPTER 12

Networking Resources

Finding Other Homeschooling Families

Your best resources are other homeschooling families. You may want to try to contact local homeschoolers. Seek out homeschoolers with similar values, and homeschoolers with similar challenges and problems. A ten minute phone call, or a brief visit, can bring quick insights and understanding to questions and concerns that are specific to your family.

How do you find homeschoolers to talk to? A local homeschooling group may be your best resource. Attend a few meetings, or take your family to some scheduled activities or field trips. If you can't find a local person listed, be sure to contact a statewide organization, where a list of local contact people is maintained. Your local librarian may know of other homeschoolers in your area, or a local midwife or La Leche League may be a worthwhile resource.

The local, state, and national groups listed below might also help to get conversations started. If you can't talk to them in person, write or call. If there is no contact for your area, consider signing up with a statewide network to be a contact and new families will be referred to you.

If you still can't find other homeschoolers, help homeschoolers find you. List yourself in the Growing Without Schooling *directory, or in the* Home Education Magazine *Support Group List. Put an ad in your local paper or post some flyers: i.e. "Parents and kids interested in homeschooling meet at the park . . ." Place a classified in* Mothering Magazine. *Buy a copy of* Teach Your

Own *and donate it to your local library. Print on the inside cover
"Donated by: " with your name and phone number. Be creative.*

*The state and local organizations, groups, and individuals
that are listed in this section are open to all, unless otherwise noted. No
inclusive group has been intentionally omitted. The philosophies and
methods espoused may vary widely from one group to another.*

*Hats off! to the volunteers who are willing to be listed as
contact people for their local areas. Please be considerate of their
generous offers of time and energy when you call, and be sure to
include a self-addressed stamped envelope when you write.*

Events, Conferences, And Curriculum Fairs

Sometimes the most helpful information about homeschooling
can be acquired at a homeschooling event. Most events are sponsored
by organizations listed in this chapter, or in Chapter 27, "Religious
Resources." Some of the Oregon organizations that have offered
events, curriculum fairs, and conferences in the past include OHEN,
OCEAN, LIGHT, and Basic Skills Assessment Service.

You might contact LIGHT, OHEN, or OCEAN for a calendar
of homeschooling events. Many state and national organizations,
including WHO and FLO in Washington, HSC in California, NHA, and
others, offer annual conferences. Call or write the organizations for
information.

Some conferences and events are for adults only, and are not
open to children. Be sure to ask, if bringing your children along is
important to you.

By the way, does the alphabet soup of all the groups and
organizations confuse you? You are neither alone nor forgotten. All of
these acronyms are explained in individual listings, below.

Statewide Networks And Organizations

It is essential that homeschoolers have some contact with a statewide organization. The rules and laws that most affect homeschoolers are created at the state level. Communication among homeschoolers on a statewide level is critical if homeschooling rights are to be preserved for all.

For that reason, all statewide organizations, regardless of affiliation, are listed in this section.

Oregon Home Education Network (OHEN)
4470 SW Hall Blvd. #286
Beaverton OR
(503)321-5166

- Statewide, non-profit, inclusive homeschooling network offering information and support to all Oregon homeschoolers. Diverse membership includes a variety of educational, religious, and political philosophies. Bi-monthly newsletter, *The Oregon Connection*, offers homeschooling information, a schedule of statewide activities, legislative and political information, resource reviews, and many submissions by members. Beginning homeschool packet is $2; membership and newsletter is $12 annually. Statewide homeschooling conference in August features workshops, speakers, panel discussions, and vendors with homeschooling resources for sale. All are welcome.

HIS Net of Oregon (Homeschool Information and Service Network Of Oregon)
PO Box 20985
Salem OR 97303
(503)699-9241

- Statewide non-profit corporation providing practical assistance to homeschool support groups and individual homeschool families. Board of directors is non-denominational Christian. HIS Net serves all homeschoolers regardless of religion or educational philosophy. Bi-monthly newsletter, *The Messenger*, contains statewide calendar of events and much more. Support group incorporation and liability insurance information is available. Computerized telephone referral service for all homeschool support groups. (For greater detail, see p. 206.)

Oregon Christian Education Association Network (OCEAN)
2515 NE 37th Ave.
Portland OR 97212
(503)288-1285

- One phone call can connect you with fundamentalist Christian homeschooling support groups anywhere in the state. (For greater detail, see p. 207.)

Oregon State Department of Education(ODE)
Leon Fuhrman, Special Education (includes homeschooling)
255 Capitol Street NE
Salem OR 97310
(503)585 (homeschool office) or (503)569-3569

Oregon State Legislature
Call 1-800-327-7389 for a copy of any bill.

Oregon Chautauqua
PO Box 80214-OC
Portland OR 97280

- Annual September gathering for unschoolers. Send SASE for information.

Oregon Association for the Talented and Gifted (OATAG)
PO Box 1703
Beaverton OR 97075
(503)629-0163

- OATAG is not a homeschooling organization but may be a valuable resource to parents of gifted children. Membership is $30, and includes a subscription to the quarterly newsletter, which offers information, activities, and resources. As John Holt said, "Every child is a gifted child..."

❖

Local Contacts and Support Groups
Listed by County

If you cannot find a local contact or group for your community below, contact a statewide, regional, or national group for help. The groups listed here are inclusive. There may be other support groups in your area that are not listed. Contact OHEN, OCEAN, or LIGHT for help in finding contacts.

Baker County

Karlynne Landrum
Mt. View Learning Center
1304 Third Street
Baker City OR 97814

Benton County

Nancy Cooke
19587 Alsea Hwy.
Alsea OR 97324
487-4002

Clackamas County

Mt. Hood Homeschoolers
622-3411

- See also Portland Metro Region

Douglas County

Craig Palermo
Reedsport
271-4024

Douglas County Homeschoolers Connection
4053 Hanna St
Roseburg OR 97470

Josephine County

The Learning Connection
Jane Joyce
PO Box 1091 #196
Grants Pass OR 97526
476-5686

- "... school-without-walls ... consulting with groups and individuals who wish to develop schools-without-walls."

Lane County

Avalos Learning Center
PO Box 70778
Eugene OR 97401

Homeschoolers of Lane County
38040 Pengra Rd
Fall Creek OR 97438
937-2271

Lane InterChristian Guild of Home Teachers (L.I.G.H.T.)
Debi Craddock
31579 Gowdyville Rd.
Cottage Grove OR 97424
942-0586

- A county-wide Christian network with 11 chapter support groups; compiles an annual all-inclusive calendar of homeschooling events; yearly Curriculum Fair. Publishes the *Oregon Homeschool Support Group Directory*, available to support group leaders for referrals only. LIGHT is open to all; board members sign a statement of faith.

Willamette Homeschoolers
Jill Hubbard and Bill Griffiths
245 West 27th Ave.
Eugene OR 97405
344-4956

- Focuses on activities for kids, with quarterly meetings to plan activities.

Linn County

Vivienne Edwards
PO Box 75
Harrisburg OR 97446
(503)995-3465 or 995-8047

Lebanon Homeschool Connection
Nancy Kaufman
30584 Hazen Ln.
Lebanon OR 97355
(503)258-2746

Marion County

Salem Homeschoolers
(503)585-3617

Multnomah County

- see Portland Metro Region, below.

Washington County

- see Portland Metro Region, below.

Yamhill County

- see Portland Metro Region, below.

Portland Metro Region

Mt. Hood Homeschoolers
(503)622-3411

- Activities and gatherings.

North Willamette Unschoolers
6501 SW Macadam
Portland OR 97202
(503)291-8493

- A homeschooling cooperative with a news bulletin listing events and gatherings of interest to unschoolers in the Portland Metro region. 10 issues/$12.

Portland Area Tri-County Homeschoolers (P.A.T.C.H.)
PO Box 82415
Portland OR 97282

- Local support and information. Publishes a newsletter every other month listing activities and news.

Regional Contacts

Sometimes the closest contact geographically or philosophically can be found in another state.

California

HomeSchool Association of California (HSC)
PO Box 231236
Sacramento CA 95823-0403
(707)765-5375

- Holds an annual conference.

Humboldt Homeschoolers
c/o Paige Smith
688 S. Westhaven Drive
Trinidad CA 95570
(707) 677-3290

Idaho

Homelearning Support Network
4120 Wisteria Way
Boise ID 83704
(208)376-7066

Washington

Clark County Home Educators (CCHE)
(206)256-9051

Columbia Basin Family Educators
Janie Levine
PO Box 300
Benton City WA 99320
(509)588-5013

- Blue Mountain region contact for eastern Oregon.

Family Learning Organization(FLO)
PO Box 7256
Spokane WA 99207-0256
(509)467-2552

- Dedicated to supporting and protecting the interests of homeschooling families throughout Washington and the Inland Northwest. Services include a Family Learning Fair.

The Moore Foundation, Raymond and Dorothy Moore
Box 1
Camas WA 98607
(206)835-2736

- Works with families to design appropriate programs for children. See Chapter 10 for an in-depth review. Christian perspective, but have worked with all for many years.

Washington Homeschool Organization (WHO)
PO Box 938
Maple Valley WA 98038

- Statewide support for Washington homeschoolers. Sponsors an annual conference for both sectarian and non-sectarian groups. An extensive curriculum exhibit is held at the conference.

❖

National Resources And Periodicals

The following list includes organizations and periodicals whose sole focus is to support homeschoolers and those groups that address the special interests or special needs of some homeschooling families. Several of well-known national resources have a Christian perspective, and may be listed here, in Chapter 27, or both. This particular listing is not alphabetical. Instead, organizations are grouped loosely with similar types of organizations as much as possible.

R Home Education Press
Mark and Helen Hegener, Publishers
PO Box 1083
Tonasket WA 98855
(509)486-1351

- Publishes: *Home Education Magazine*(HEM), reviewed in Chapter 10, *Alternatives in Education, The Homeschool Reader, Good Stuff, I Learn Better By Teaching Myself*, a number of helpful, inexpensive booklets, and more.

R Holt Associates/ Growing Without Schooling (GWS)
2269 Massachusetts Ave.
Cambridge MA 02140
(617)864-3100

- Publishes *Growing Without Schooling*, which is reviewed in Chapter 10. Originally started by John Holt. Many resources, books, ideas, and connections are available through this organization.

National Homeschool Association (NHA)
PO Box 15790
Cincinnati OH 45215-7290
(513)772-9580

- National homeschool organization. Publishes the *Forum*, a quarterly newsletter, and travel directory. Sponsors an annual conference. An info packet is available for $3.00. Family membership is $15.00 a year.

R The Drinking Gourd
PO Box 2557
Redmond WA 98073
(206)836-0336

- A homeschooling magazine and resource catalog that explores home education from different perspectives, with particular attention to the issues that affect people of color. Six issues for $15, and twelve issues for $25. Includes a bookstore of multi-cultural resources.

Umoja-Unidad-United, A Newsletter for Homeschoolers of Color
Kristin Cleage Williams
5621 South Lakeshore Drive
Idlewild MI 49642

- A new newsletter that will cover both Latina/o and Black homeschoolers... and anyone else who identifies themselves as a person or family of color, regardless of other factors that keep us apart. Subscriptions will run about $10 per year. This newsletter depends on articles and letters from the readers!

Harmony Network
PO Box 75
Harrisburg OR 97446
(503)995-3465

- A multi-cultural, multi-faith network of parents participating in, and taking responsibility for, their children's education. Six issues/year for $10.00.

Unschooling Ourselves
PO Box 1014
Eugene OR 97440

- A newsletter that continues the work begun in Grace Llewellyn's *The Teenage Liberation Handbook*; "a way to build energy and community among my readers." Also open to teachers and former teachers who are rethinking their careers. Discover how unschooling works. $12 for four issues.

Wisconsin Parents Association
PO Box 2502
Madison WI 53701

- WPA is Wisconsin's inclusive statewide homeschooling association. WPA has thoughtful state coverage of national
  legislation issues, as well as a good understanding of what a
  reasonable homeschooling law should be. Offers an important political perspective to the often confusing politics of
  homeschooling. Annual membership of $20 gets you on the
  mailing list.

R NATional cHallenged Homeschoolers Association (NATHHAN)
Tom and Sherry Bushnell
5383 Alpine Rd. SE
Olalla WA98359
(206)857-4257

- The only resource I know of whose sole purpose is to help
  families to homeschool children who have learning or physical challenges. Willing to help anyone. Newsletter. Workshops available.

Washington Homeschool Research Project
Jon Wartes
16109 NE 169 Place
Woodinville WA 98072

Canadian Alliance of Home Schoolers
195 Markville Road
Unionville, Ontario, L3R 4V8
Canada

- Provides information, support and advocacy for Canadian
  home educators.

Children and Communities Network
c/o Lynne Knowles
14556 Little Greenhorn Road
Grass Valley CA 95945
(916)272-2856

- Communicate with other unschoolers, homeschoolers, alternative schoolers, etc. Send information about yourself plus
  $5 and get a biography of others in return.

Home Educators Computer Users Group
2684 Howard Chapel Dr.
Damascus MD 20872-1247
(301)253-5467

Single Parents Educating Children in Alternative Learning (SPECIAL)
2 Pineview Drive #5
Amelia OH 45102

- Single parents have found creative ways to homeschool their children, including home business, care assistance, and co-homeschooling. S.P.E.C.I.A.L. welcomes people of all races and beliefs, and membership, on a sliding scale from $12 to $20 per year, includes the newsletter, resources, and a directory.

Homeschoolers for Peace
PO Box 74
Midpines CA 95345

Homeschoolers Travel Network
PO Box 58746
Seattle WA 98138-1746
(206)432-1544

Vegan Homeschoolers
5313 A Heritage Way NE
Albuquerque NM 87109

The Frugal Times
Rt. 1 Box 173
Cherryvale KS 67335

- A monthly newsletter that is full of tips on ways to save money, time, and energy. The goal is to "...help families everywhere get a lot more out of what they have." Twelve issues, 96 pages, $12.

Living Cheap News
PO Box 700058
San Jose CA 95170

- A monthly newsletter that advocates frugality, oriented toward the urban/suburban reader. $12/year.

The Penny Pincher
PO Box 809
Kings Park NY 11754

- "For people who want to save dollars." A bi-monthly 12 page newsletter full of information on ways to save money. $15 per year subscription.

Tightwad Gazette
Rural Route 1, Box 3570
Leeds ME 04263

- A monthly newsletter that advocates frugality. $12/year.

Mothers at Home
8310A Old Courthouse Road
Vienna VA 22182
(800)783-4666

- Magazine providing an opportunity for at-home mothers to share feelings and insights.

Message Post
POB 190
Philomath OR 97370

- Portable dwelling info-letter. Six issues/$5, sample issue/$1.

Resource People

Some families have concerns or interests that are unique. It is beyond the scope of this handbook to provide all the resources available for every special need or interest, but there are many people out there who are willing to share what they know.

An excellent way to contact such people, or to become a contact person, is through *Growing Without Schooling*. Once each year the editors update and publish an extensive list of resource people. The most recent issue that I have seen includes lists of professionals, including certified teachers; lawyers; professors; psychologists; cooperative school districts; and, interestingly, grown-up homeschoolers.

In addition, the most recent *GWS* list of resource people includes people who have had homeschooling experience with the following subjects: adoption; blindness; ham radio; home computers; learning disabilities; Montessori; physical handicaps; single parents; traveling families; twins; custody disputes; Down syndrome; autism.

❖

Alternative Education

The following organizations address the overlapping interests and needs of both homeschoolers and alternative schools.

Alliance for Parental Involvement in Education, Inc. (ALLPIE)
9 Kinderhook St.
Chatham NY 12037
(518)392-4277

- Provides support for parents concerning to their children's education. Newsletter, referral service, workshops, book catalog, conferences.

Alternative Education Resource Organization (AERO)
417 Roslyn Road
Roslyn Heights NY 11577
(516)621-2195

- Provides good coverage of both homeschooling and alternative education news. Jerry Mintz, publisher, has worked with Russian educators in developing new alternative types of schools in Russia. $10/year.

FairTest - National Center for Fair & Open Testing
342 Broadway
Cambridge MA 02139-1802
(617)864-4810, FAX (617)487-2224

- Provides information and research about testing. Quarterly subscription, $15.

Holistic Education Review
39 Pearl Street
Brandon VT 05733-1007
(802)247-8312

Learning Unlimited Network of Oregon (LUNO)
Gene Lehman
31960 SE Chin St.
Boring OR 97009
(503)663-5153

- An eclectic newsletter that includes a variety of information, opinions on the state of education in America, phonics and language activities, and more.

National Coalition of Alternative Community Schools
PO Box 15036
Sante Fe NM 87506
(505)474-4312

- National support for alternative education, includes section on homeschooling. Holds conferences. Network of parent cooperatives, free schools, homeschoolers.

Network of Progressive Educators
PO Box 6028
Evanston Il 60204

- Organization for private, public, open, and progressive educators.

Private Education Issues
Charles J. O'Malley & Associates
4301 Adrienne Drive
Alexandria VA 22309
(703)779-5929, Fax (703)799-5930

- O'Malley has been a major policy advisor on private education-related issues (including homeschooling) to three U.S. Secretaries of Education.

Skole (pronounced sko-lay)
72 Philip Street
Albany NY 12202

- The journal of alternative education.

Washington Alternative Learning Association
Bob Fizzell (Executive Liaison)
1201 NW 109th St.
Vancouver WA 98685
(206)574-4017

There is no use whatever trying to help people
who do not help themselves. You cannot push anyone up a ladder
unless he be willing to climb himself.
—ANDREW CARNEGIE

Part Three

Curriculum
Resources

An education
isn't how much you have committed to memory,
or even how much you know. It's being able to differentiate
between what you do know and what you don't.
—ANATOLE FRANCE

CHAPTER 13

Curriculum Programs And Assistance

Commercial curriculums and correspondence schools meet the needs of some homeschooling families. Planning services can help you plan an individualized program for your children. Look for programs that can be incorporated into a homeschooling schedule that suits your family. If you want still more choices, look through the Chapter 27 where there are many curriculum packages and services with a Christian perspective. You may also want to look through Chapter 16 for textbook suppliers.

For high school and college age students, you will find additional programs and resources listed separately in Chapter 14.

Oregon

Ann Lahrson Homeschool Services
PO Box 80214-AL
Portland OR 97280
(503)244-9677

- Private consultation; achievement testing; curriculum planning; selected books for sale; referrals. Workshops on various topics, including: curriculum planning; basics of homeschooling; unschooling; visual math. Student classes.

Custom Curriculum Company, "Materials for Learning with Joy"
owned by the David Curl family
76504 Poplar Street
Oakridge OR 97463
782-2571

- Services and materials for historic unit studies. Customized curriculums are developed during a one day consultation, Over 5000 titles, including books, games, kits, and cassettes, are offered for purchase. Send $2.00 for a catalog. Unit study guide available for Oregon History. Workshops on subjects of interest, particularly with respect to unit studies. Open Wed. 9 am till noon. Will work with all.

Family Learning Services
1755 Graham Drive
Eugene OR 97405
686-0851

- Individual curriculum planning for preschool through high school are based on learning style, ability, and the needs of each student. Students completing the high school program receive a diploma. Provides achievement testing services. Christian perspective; works with all.

The Learning Connection
Jane Joyce
PO Box 1091 #196
Grants Pass OR 97526
476-5686

- A private non-accredited school (K-12 plus Experimental College). Combines home learning with private schooling in a "school without walls." TLC students keep a daily learning log of activities. Materials advice, feedback and encouragement, along with social and community opportunities.

Sharon Rocha
22650 NW Moran Rd.
Hillsboro OR 97214
241-3412

- Services to homeschooling families including: achievement testing, identification of learning and teaching styles, and curriculum development.

Cascade Education Conservatory
Christine Webb, M. A. T.
Portland OR
245-7430

- "Empowering families through education, information, and dialogue." Academic planning, portfolio development, assessment and testing, tutoring services, workshops, and individual consultations.

National

American School
850 East 58th Street
Chicago IL 60637
(312)947-3300

- A traditional, accredited, long-established correspondence high school program.

Calvert School
105 Tuscany Road
Baltimore MD 21210
(301)243-6031

- Calvert is a long established correspondence program for students in families living abroad, child actors, and others who could not attend traditional school. The program is packaged, classical, and includes books, tests, materials and supplies. K-8.

Clonlara School
Pat Montgomery, Ph.D., Director
Home Based Education Program
1289 Jewett
Ann Arbor MI 48104
(313)769-4515

- Clonlara's homeschool outreach program will assist families in designing their own curriculum. They also provide a good support system and have information about requirements in each state. Director Pat Montgomery is a long time supporter of alternative education and is an active member of the National Homeschool Association. Grants a recognized diploma.

Hampton Educational Center
12000 Wabana Lake Road
Grand Rapids MN 55744-9200

- Consultation services. The student and family are evaluated through a questionnaire, and individualized recommendations are made for learning resources that are tailored to the child's needs and to the family's situation, lifestyle, and beliefs. Hampton is not affiliated with any product supplier. Thousands of educational products have been field tested. Clients purchase recommended resources directly from suppliers, not through Hampton.

Laurel Springs School
PO Box 1440
Ojai CA 93024
(805)646-8213

- A private school offering independent study programs for kindergarten through eighth grade. Support services include seminars, newsletters, educational consultants, assessment and record maintenance, and teacher support. Offers Oak Meadow curriculum among other curricular choices.

L-CIPSSI Curriculum Services
26801 Pine Ave.
Bonita Springs FL 33923
(813)992-6381, FAX (813)992-6473

- L-CIPSSI customizes homeschool curriculum packages based on pre-screened consumable work-texts. Provides schedule, guidelines, and teacher supplies. Grade oriented.

HOMER (HOMe Education Resource Network)
IMSATT
105 West Broad St.
Falls Church VA 22046
(703)533-7500

- On-line courseware for your Apple Macintosh or PC compatible computer, available through Internet or Compuserve. Will include Calvert K-8; CYBIS, elementary through college level courses; other curricula may also come available if publishers are willing to convert courses. Educational institutions may add both college and high school courses. A brochure and a trial kit are available.

The Moore Foundation, Raymond and Dorothy Moore
Box 1
Camas WA 98607
(206)835-2736

- Offers several homeschooling programs. Sells educational books and curriculum items and programs. The Moores are proponents of the "Moore Homeschooling Formula" - a balance of study, work, and service. Christian perspective, but open to all.

Oak Meadow
PO Box 712
Blacksburg VA 94063
(703)552-3263

- Oak Meadow publishes a well known and highly praised packaged curriculum based on the Waldorf philosophy. It includes a syllabus, supplemental books and materials. Oak Meadow also provides support services - teacher support, school enrollment, if desired, and a diplomaprogram.

Pinewood School
112 Road D.
Pine CO 80470
(303)838-4418
Olivia Loria, Director

- The school's purpose is to individualize the learning process. Pinewood offers nine services to homeschoolers: a home-based education program, an enrollment only program, a diploma program, consultation, a test filing service, a tutoring service, units of study, workshops, and on-line computer services. Diplomas are offered either through a traditional Carnegie Credit Program or Pinewood's Competency-Based Method. Accredited by the National Association for the Legal Support of Alternative Schools.

Upattinas School Open Community Corp.
429 Greenridge Rd.
Glenmore PA 19343
(215)458-5138

- Upattinas is a long standing alternative school with a national reputation. Its homeschool outreach program provides support with curriculum development, dealing with school districts, books, testing, portfolio evaluation, etc.

Under the Apple Tree
Apple Tree Press
PO Box 8
Woodinville WA 98072

- Hard to classify this bi-monthly publication, but it seems useful to parents wanting help with curriculum planning by mail. Could be very useful in developing unit studies. It is packed with seasonal and theme ideas similar to those used by good elementary classroom teachers, but focused toward the homeschooler. Hands on, activity oriented ideas - could provide a real boost when you are out of ideas. Each issue focuses on a theme, with activities in all subject areas. $18/year, $34/two years. Sample copy, $3; back issues, $5.

CHAPTER 14

High School, College, And Apprenticeships

Some young people want traditional learning experiences outside of the traditional school environment. The following list includes information about books, programs, and apprenticeships for high school and college students.

The program section lists schools and businesses that offer correspondence school programs, curriculum packages, teacher support, skill evaluation, and/or diploma programs.

Some students seek assistance in finding unusual or non-traditional learning paths. Both Clonlara and Pinewood Schools (listed below) offer alternative paths to high school diplomas. Information about apprenticeships is included at the end of the chapter.

❖

Correspondence Schools And Programs

American School
850 East 58th Street
Chicago IL 60637
(312)947-3300

- A traditional, accredited, correspondence high school program. Diploma granted.

The Center for the Advancement of Education Programs for Higher Education
3301 College Ave.
Ft. Lauderdale FL 33314
(305)475-7380

- Publishes a two hundred fifty page directory listing 105 alternatives from 46 states, entitled Tomorrow's Innovations Today: Exemplary Alternative Education Programs

Clonlara School
Home Based Education Program
1289 Jewett
Ann Arbor MI 48104
(313)769-4515
Pat Montgomery, Ph.D. Director

- Clonlara's homeschool outreach program will assist families in designing their own curriculum. They also provide a good support system and have information about requirements in each state. Director Pat Montgomery is a long time supporter of alternative education and is an active member of the National Homeschool Association. Grants a recognized diploma.

College-Level Examination Program (CLEP)
DANTES
Advanced Placement Program (APP)
Program Director, College Level Examinations
College Board
Princeton NJ 08541

- These exams can be taken by people of any age and test knowledge gained through nontraditional methods.

Family Learning Services
1755 Graham Drive
Eugene OR 97405
686-0851

- Individual curriculum planning and recommendations for preschool through high school are based on learning style, abilities, and needs of each student. Christian - will work with all. Students completing the high school program receive a diploma. Provides achievement testing services.

Indiana University
Bloomington IN
(800)334-1011

- More than 100 independent study high school courses; 200 accredited university-level courses are available through independent study. Call for a free bulletin.

The Learning Connection
Jane Joyce
PO Box 1091 #196
Grants Pass OR 97526
476-5686

- A private, non-accredited school (K-12 plus Experimental College). Combines home learning with private schooling in a "school without walls." TLC students keep a daily learning log of activities. Materials advice, feedback and encouragement, social and community opportunities.

National Home Study Council
1601 18th Street, NW
Washington DC 20009

- If you seek an accredited school at the high school level or beyond, send for the Directory.

Oak Meadow
PO Box 712
Blacksburg VA 94063
(703)552-3263

- Oak Meadow publishes a well known curriculum, which includes a syllabus along with supplemental books and materials. School enrollment and a diploma program are offered.

Pinewood School
Olivia Loria, Director
112 Road D.
Pine CO 80470
(303)838-4418

- Pinewood offers nine services to homeschoolers: a home-based education program, an enrollment only program, a diploma program, consultation, a test filing service, a tutoring service, units of study, workshops, and on-line computer services. Diplomas are offered via traditional Carnegie Credit Program or Pinewood's Competency-Based Method. Accredited.

University of California Extension
High School Correspondence Courses
Berkeley CA 94720

University of Nebraska Independent Study High School
Continuing Ed Center, Rm 269
Lincoln NE 68583

- A correspondence school that grants a recognized diploma.

University of the State of New York
Cultural Education Center
Albany NY 12230

- A widely recognized external degree program. Also runs the Regents Credit Bank.

University Without Walls
Union for Experimenting Colleges and Universities
Yellow Springs OH 45387

- An alternative plan for undergraduate work. Students identify their own educational needs and learn to satisfy them with the help of guidance teachers and advisors. Write for information.

❖

Apprenticeship Programs

Apprentice Alliance
151 Potrero Ave.
San Francisco CA 94103
(415)863-8661

- This organization maintains a directory of potential apprenticeships in the arts, business, and the trades. Apprentices pay an annual $25 registration fee and a $100 placement fee for each successful apprenticeship. Directories can be purchased for $5, plus a $1 shipping fee.

Center of Interim Programs
PO Box 2347
Cambridge MA 02238
(617)547-0980

- This center, run by Cornelius Bull, has thousands of options. They start by getting to know you, your interests and your finances, and then work with you to find an appropriate placement.

The Foundation for Field Research
Alpine CA
(619)445-9264

- Helps match volunteers with botanists, archaeologists, primatologists, and other researchers.

Maine Organic Farmers & Gardeners Association
Farm Apprentice Placement Service
Box 2176
Augusta ME 04338-2176
(207)622-3118

- Helps place apprentices with master farmers and gardeners, who teach what they know, and offer room and board in exchange for farm work. For men and women 18 years or older. $20 registration fee.

The Mentor Connection
Linda Silrum at Metro ECSU
3499 Lexington Ave. N.
St. Paul MN 55126
(612)490-0058

- A program for high school students in the metropolitan St.
  Paul area that allows them to learn advanced skills associated with a profession. A helpful model for anyone who
  wants to establish a mentorship program.

National Society for Internships and Experiential Education
Sally Migliore, Project Director
3509 Haworth Drive, Suite 207
Raleigh NC 27609
(919)787-3263

- Has active groups in each state.

New Alchemy Institute
237 Hatchville Rd.
East Falmouth MA 02536

- Offers internships.

Time Out
619 E. Blithedale Ave., Suite C
Mill Valley CA 94941
(415)383-1834

- David Denman helps you identify your priorities and goals
  and then researches individually appropriate opportunities.
  He helps arrange opportunities and then stays in touch with
  his clients.

Books

These books may help you and your teen-ager reach decisions about high school, careers, and college. Unless otherwise noted, the books are available through your local library, inter-library loan, John Holt's Book and Music Store Catalog, Home Education Press, or your local book merchant. Additional books that you may find useful may be found under specific subjects such as Math or Language Arts.

Alternatives in Education, edited by Mark and Helen Hegener. Includes an informative chapter on high school and higher education.

The Cambridge Pre-GED Program. NY: Cambridge Book Co.

Careers and Colleges, from Home Education Press. $2.00 postpaid. Reprint of several articles from *Home Education Magazine*.

College Admissions: A Guide for Homeschoolers, by Judy Gelner. 1988. Poppyseed Press, Box 85, Sedalia CO 80135. One family's experiences plus some general information.

Cracking the System: The SAT, by Adam Robinson and John Katzman. NY: Willard, 1986. Excellent guide to preparing for the SAT.

Do The Right Things! Office of Publications, Grinnell College, PO Box 805, Grinnell IA 50112. Help with college selection. Free.

Earn College Credit for What You Know, by Susan Simosko. Washington DC: Acropolis Books, 1985.

Home Study Opportunities: The Complete Guide to Going to School by Mail, by Laurie M. Carlson. While Hall VA: Betterway, 1989.

*How to Get the Degree You Want: Bear's Guide to Non-Traditional College Degree*s, by John Bear. Berkeley CA: Ten Speed Press, updated yearly.

Internships: 38,000 On-the-Job Training Opportunities for Students and Adults. Cincinnati: Writer's Digest, 1989.

The National Directory of Internships, available for $22 plus shipping and handling, from National Society for Internships and Experiential Education, 3509 Haworth Drive, Suite 207, Raleigh NC 27609-7229, (919)787-3263. Thousands of opportunities in 75 fields for college, graduate, and high school students as well as for people who are not in school.

Passing the GED. Glenview IL: Scott, Foresman.

Peterson's Independent Study Catalog. Listing of hundreds of academic courses on the high school, college, and graduate level.

The Question is College: Guiding Your Child to the Right Choices after High School, by Herbert Kohl. NY: Random House, 1989.

Real Lives: eleven teenagers who don't go to school, by Grace Llewellyn. Order from Lowry House, Box 1014, Eugene OR 97440. $16.95 postpaid. Personal stories by teens about how they educate themselves without formal schooling.

The Teenage Liberation Handbook: how to quit school and get a real life and education, by Grace Llewellyn. Order from Lowry House, Box 1014, Eugene OR 97440. $16.95 postpaid. Written for teenagers who are looking for alternatives, and the book is full of information. A good read for any homeschooler looking for new ideas.

What Color Is Your Parachute? A Practical Manual for Job-Hunters and Career Changers, by Richard Bolles. Berkeley CA: Ten Speed Press.

The Whole Work Catalog, Box 297-UE, Boulder CO 80306. Catalog of books about work; many alternatives.

CHAPTER 15

Instructional Materials Catalogs

Wishbooks for homeschoolers! This is an inexpensive resource that everyone can enjoy, no matter what philosophy or program you choose to use. Write for a few of these catalogs and get a bigger picture of what's "out there." These catalogs can be used in so many ways: ideas for learning materials you can make yourself, teaching tips for difficult concepts, book reviews, good examples of concise writing, colorful pictures to cut out, and, oh yes, you can order really great stuff! Essential for families designing their own curriculums. A wide variety of materials for all subject areas can be found in these catalogs. Other catalogs are listed under specific subject headings in Part Three, and in Part Four, Religious Resources.

Activity Resources Co. Inc.
PO Box 4875
Hayward CA 94540
(415)782-1300, FAX (415)782-8172

- Carries a variety of math manipulatives, books, etc.

Animal Town
PO Box 485
Healdsburg CA 95448
(800)445-8642

- Quality cooperative, non-competitive games, tapes, and more. For families that like to learn through play.

Aristoplay
PO Box 7529
Ann Arbor MI 48107
(800)634-7738

- Excellent collection of "games for fun and learning."

Bits and Pieces
1 Puzzle Place B8016
Stevens Point WI 54481-7199

- Fun catalog of quality puzzles, models and gifts.

Bluestocking Press/
Educational Spectrums
PO Box 1014
Placerville CA 95667
(916)621-1123

- Homeschooler-oriented catalog. Mostly social studies. Many hard-to-find Laura Ingalls Wilder related items.

Bueno
In One Ear Publications
29481 Manzanita
Campo CA 91906

- This magazine/catalog is full of "Friendly Foreign Language Learning." Language learning materials are reviewed and sold. Articles and recipes in Spanish. $8/year.

Child's Work/Child's Play
PO Box 1586
King of Prussia PA 19406
(800)962-1141

- Products designed to teach values, self-confidence, and courage.

Chinaberry Book Service
2830 Via Orange Way, Suite B
Spring Valley CA 92078

- The catalog itself is great reading, and the recommendations come from the heart of the reviewer. A quality selection of books for both parents and children.

Cuisenaire Co. of America
12 Church St., Box D
New Rochelle NY 10805
(800)237-3142, (914)235-0900
FAX (914)576-3480

- Colorful catalog with lots of quality math and science manipulatives. Terrific materials that can be used throughout the school years.

Dover Publications
31 East Second St.
Mineola NY 11501

- Many items for $1. Lists books on many subjects, but especially arts and crafts. Large selection of children's activity books, coloring books, paper doll books, postcard books.

Educators Publishing Service, Inc.
75 Moulton St.
Cambridge MA 02138-1104

- Traditional materials. Mostly workbooks, etc., on phonics, reading, history, remedial reading, and learning disability books and materials.

Hearthsong
2211 Blucher Valley Rd.
Sebastopol CA 95472
(800)533-4397

- High quality natural-material supplies, dolls, and learning aids, generally of the Waldorf or Montessori type.

Heartleaf - Homemade Music, Art & Movement
Box 40
Slocan Park BC VOG 2EO
Canada

- Lovely newspaper style catalog of books, tapes, etc., "to encourage everyone to be active in the arts." Published by a homeschooling family.

History Alive Through Music
Hear and Learn Publications
603 SE Morrison Rd.
Vancouver WA 98664
(206)694-0034

- Cassette tapes (with books) of songs from American history.

The Homeschool Exchange
17819 Beall Rd. SW
Vashon Island WA98070
Jan Slater, Publisher

- Not a catalog at all, but a newsletter through which you can buy and sell curriculum and educational resources. Subscriptions are $7.50/annually for 6 bimonthly issues. Advertise your used curriculum and resources for sale, or buy used at very reasonable prices.

Home School Supply House
PO Box 7
Fountain Green UT 84632
(800)772-3129

- Catalog designed with the homeschooling family in mind. A variety of materials for many styles of learning.

In Print for Children
2113 Kenmore Ave.
Glenside PA 19038

- Quality Montessori posters and cards.

Jetco Publications, Dept. TFK
Box 85
Livingston NJ 07039-0085

- Not a catalog, but a book listing many free things you can send away for, from a replica of a million dollar gold certificate to a presidential fitness award. If you don't get what you send for, the book's authors will send you a free copy of next year's revised book. $2.50.

John Holt's Book and Music Store
Holt Associates
2269 Massachusetts Ave.
Cambridge MA 02140

- Lots of good quality materials in many subjects that are useful with an individualized or unschooled model of homeschooling. offered especially for homeschoolers.

Lakeshore Curriculum Materials Co.
2695 E. Domingez St.
PO Box 6261
Carson CA 90749
(800)421-5354

- Colorful and slick, traditional school-type wish catalog, with lots of manipulatives. Good descriptions and colorful pictures give a good preview of what is offered.

Meadowbook Press
18218 Minnetonka Blvd.
Deephaven MN 55391

- Not a catalog, but a compilation of free resources you can write for on topics like tourism, hobbies, sports and games. Cost $4.95 from booksellers or $6.20 postpaid.

Michael Olaf's Essential Montessori
PO Box 1162
Arcata CA 95521
(707)826-1557

- Very nice catalog of Montessori and other materials, appropriate for homeschoolers. We have found a lot of treasures.

Montessori Store
PO Box B
Sebastopol CA 95473-0601
(800)325-2502

- Good source of creative play and natural art materials.

Music and Moments with the Masters
Cornerstone Curriculum Project
2006 Flat Creek Place
Richardson TX 75080

- Cassette programs about composers.

Music For Little People
PO Box 1460
Redway CA 95560
(800)727-2233

- The best music catalog we've come across. Cassettes, videos, musical instruments. More than music.

Nasco
901 Janesville Ave.
Ft. Atkinson WI 53538
(800)558-9595

- Wide selection of teaching materials and supplies for educators. Traditional style catalog.

National Women's History Project
7738 Bell Road
Windsor CA 95492-8518

- A good resource, with many materials that are not available elsewhere. Even the catalog teaches things not commonly known about women's history. Free catalog.

The Reading Child
PO Box 1880
Evanston IL 60204-1880

- "A catalog of outstanding literature for children who can read." Good reviews of books offered.

Scientific Wizardry Educational Products
9925 Fairview Ave.
Boise ID 83704
(208)377-8575

- Free catalog. Science materials; quality learning items.

Tellurian Travellers
4412 Colver Rd.
Phoenix OR 97535
(800)950-5505

- Educational items—Bob Books, games, puzzles, nature.

The Timberdoodle
E. 1510 Spencer Lake Rd.
Shelton WA 98584

- Small catalog with an emphasis on "hands-on materials and things out of the ordinary." Said to have the best price on Cuisenaire rods anywhere. Fischertechnik, Wrap-ups, Koosh, Klutz, and Lauri. Owned by a homeschool family.

Trans Tech
Creative Learning Systems
16510 Via Esprilo
San Diego CA 92127
(800)458-2880

- "Making technology transparent at school/home/work/play." Many interesting science, math, and technical materials.

Zephyr Press
3316 N Chapel Ave, PO Box 13448 - C
Tucson AZ 85732-3448
(602)322-5090

- Many popular modern teaching materials.

If a man empties his purse into his head,
no man can take it away from him. An investment in knowledge
always pays the best interest.
--BENJAMIN FRANKLIN

CHAPTER 16

Textbook Resources

If you want to use the same textbooks that are used in public schools, the textbook representatives in Oregon may be able to help. Students who plan to re-enter public school may want to use the same texts that are used in the classrooms.

Northwest Textbook Depository
17970 SW McEvans
Portland OR
639-3193

- A place where you can order textbooks, if you know what you want. No showroom. Order six or more and get school prices. (You cannot get Saxon math books from them.)

Oregon Textbook Representatives
3913 NE Royal Court
Portland OR 97232
235-2521

- The representatives on the following pages are generally willing to send homeschoolers catalogs of their materials, and to help you in any way they can. Some require "proof" of homeschooling before allowing you to purchase teacher editions.

Addison-Wesley
Jerry McReal
8625-B Curry Drive
Wilsonville 97070
694-5979
(800) 548-4885

Amsco School Publications, Inc.
Dean Irvin
12820 SW 6th
Beaverton 97005
626-2896

Casio, Inc.
Calculator Products Division
Joy Muhs
10331 Shirley Avenue
Northridge, CA 91326
(818) 360-8457

Delta Education
John Klug
14400 SW 27th Court
Beaverton 97005
646-0381
(800)258-1302

Ed-Tex (K-Adult)
Rusty Carter
21113 SW 86th Court
Tualatin 97062
692-0671
(800) 898-3340

EMC Publishing
Dave Hodge
10647 NE 133rd Place
Kirkland WA 98034
(206) 821-4523
(800) 328-1452

**Everyday Learning
Corporation**
(University of Chicago Math -
Elem.)
Vince Coleman
8440 SW Murdock St.
Tigard 97224-7337
620-4571
(800) 328-1452

Glencoe Division
Macmillan-McGraw-Hill Grades
7-12
(Includes all Glencoe,
Macmillan/Mcgraw-Hill, Merrill,
Gregg secondary programs, and
all Houghton Mifflin Business
Ed.)

Nick Sinnott
5582 SW Natchez
Tualatin 97062
691-9316
(800) 452-6126

**Harcourt Brace Jovanovich,
Inc./Holt**
Carol Slegers
3130 NW 148th Place
Beaverton 97006
629-8522
(800) 426-6577

D. C. Heath & Co.
Polly Holbrook
15200 NW Burlington Court
Portland 97231
621-3925
(800) 2385-9838

Holt, Rinehart & Winston, Inc.
Harcourt, Brace and
Jovanovich, Inc.
(HRW will now distribute all
Harcourt, Brace, Jovanovich and
Holt, Rinehart and Winston
secondary school programs 7-12)
(See HBJ for elementary school
programs.)

Frederic Juras
26085 NE Butteville Road
Aurora 97002
682-1629
(800) 228-4658

Houghton Mifflin Co.
Harlan Heyden - Elementary
Division (Grades K-8)
245 Kashmir Court SE
Salem 97306
371-1353
(800) 222-8460

Karen DeDonato - Secondary
Division (Grades 9-12)
6831 NE Broadway
Portland 97213
254-3764
(800) 222-8460

Jamestown
Susan Campbell
3610 NE Peerless
Portland 97213
233-2069

Macmillan/McGraw-Hill
(Includes Scribner, Laidlaw,
Merrill, Bowmar-Noble, and
Economy K-8 programs)
James "Rusty" Slay
21675 SW Hedges Drive
Tualatin 97062
692-5011

McDougal, Littell & Co.
James Genereaux
4851 N Loftus Road
Florence 97439
997-2885
(800) 424-3077

Modern Curriculum Press
Janet Johnson
940 NW Culbertson Drive
Seattle WA 98177
(206) 448-6421
(800) 321-3106

National Textbook Co.
Tom Trier
11433 Ranchta Dr.
Los Altos, CA 95024
(415) 390-0280

Optical Data Corporation
Pete Reeder
12538 SE 210th Court
Kent WA 98031
(206) 630-8669
(800) 524-2481
(206) 630-8667 (FAX)

Open Court Pulishing Co.
M.J. (Marijane) Brown
6612 Montana Lane
Vancouver, WA 98661
(206) 737-6464
(800) 435-6850
315 Fifth St.
Peru, IL 61354
(800) 435-6850

Perma-Bound
Jamie Orlowski / Phillip Orlowski
935 SE 54th Street
Portland 97215
236-6805

PSU Continuing Education Publications
Tena Spears
PO Box 1394
Portland 97207
725-4846

Prentice-Hall, Inc.
Tim Oberg
0027 SE Clatsop St,
Portland 97266
777-8606
(800) 677-1223, ext. 7914

Saxon Publishers
Jerry Hong
145 Doud Street
Blackfoot ID 83221
(208) 522-3791 (Work)
(208) 529-0827 (Home)
(800) 284-7019

Scholastics, Inc.
Creig Ross
1945 NW Lantana Drive
Corvallis 97330
752-3000

Scott, Foresman & Co.
Tod Diamond
12162 SW Schools Ferry Rd.
#160
Tigard 97223
639-8084
(800) 554-4411

Silver Burdett & Ginn
Linda C. Dubois
8702 NE 42nd Court
Beaverton 97007
576-4968
(800) 677-1223 Ext.5862

South-Western Publishing Co.
Jim Briggs / Gary Kranc
4770 Duke Dr. Suite 200
Mason, OH 45040
(800) 543-7972

Sundance Publishers & Distributers
Gail Sutton
15155 SW Daphne Court
Beaverton 97404
641-4531
(800) 727-0564

Zaner-Bloser, Inc.
Lydia Graffis
786 Fremont Avenue
Eugene 97404
689-4310

CHAPTER 17
Language Arts

Reading, writing, spelling, literature, grammar, dramatics, speaking, listening. The best language activities are the easiest and most natural.

Talk with your children. Listen to them. Read to and with them. Discuss what you read. Write to and with them. Let them write letters to Grandma and to their pen pals. Make up and perform plays. Tell stories. Go to the library. Buy books. Teach children to use tape and video recorders to record their own work. Play Scrabble, Mad Libs, Word Yahtzee, and other word games.

Leave a dictionary and a thesaurus around for easy access and discovery. Be sure to have lots of paper and writing implements, and be willing to spell the words your child asks for, and help them find strategies for spelling words for themselves. If you want some structured curriculum, try some of the materials listed below, or thumb through your favorite general curriculum catalog.

Materials And Resources

Sometimes you need a program or book to get you started, or to keep you going. The following list provides a starting point. In fact, some of the books below are excellent resources for writers, readers, and word lovers of any age.

A Book of Puzzlements: Play and Invention With Language by Herbert Kohl. Schocken Books.

- If you enjoy word play, and want to use play and games to teach the elements of language and literature, this book will keep you busy for some time. Grammar, sentence structure, poetry, figures of speech, codes, vocabulary, language logic, riddles, fables, proverbs, and more.

Alpha Phonics
Paradigm
Box 45161
Boise ID 83711

- A primer for beginning readers.

Book-Write: a creative bookmaking guide for young authors
Michelle O'Brien-Palmer
MicNik Publications
PO Box 3041
Kirkland WA 98072

- A user-friendly book for children that offers several strategies for pre-writing, editing, publishing, and book construction. Respectful, useful instruction for young authors.

Calligraphy for the Beginner, by Tom Gourdie. Taplinger Publishing.

- For those who want to create letters, not just "handwrite."

Legible Handwriting
Continuing Education Publications
Portland State University, Dept. T.
PO Box 1394
Portland OR 97207

- Pencil (not pen and ink) italic handwriting program.

National Association for Young Writers, Inc.
PO Box 3000, Dept. YW
Denville NJ 07834

- Non-profit group working with children to improve writing skills and enhance creative development. Publishes directory of writing professionals.

Parents Who Love Reading, Kids Who Don't, by Mary Leonhardt.

- Realistic look at why some kids hate to read and what parents and teachers can do to help. Public school perspective but lots of at-home suggestions.

Play 'n Talk
7105 Manzanita St.
Carlsbad CA 92009
(619)438-4330

- Spelling program. Recorded lessons, riddles, games, syllable slides.

Playing Shakespeare
Aristoplay
PO Box 7529
Ann Arbor MI 48107-7529
(800)634-7738

- A board game of Shakespearean charades for ages 12 and up. No special knowledge of Shakespeare's plays is necessary.

Shoe Tree: The Literary Magazine by and for Young Writers
PO Box 3000, Dept. YW
Denville NJ 07834

- Subscriptions available from National Association for Young Writers (above). Article and art submissions to Sheila Cowing, Editor, NAYW, 215 Valle del Sol Drive, Santa Fe NM 87501.

Spelling Instruction That Makes Sense
Jo Phenix and Doreen Scott-Dunne
Pembroke Publishers Limited
528 Hood Road
Markham, Ontario L3R 3K9
Canada

- A useful book for parents who want to have something in their hands to help with spelling. Also useful for the older student who struggles with spelling.

Real Toads in Imaginary Gardens, Stephen Phillip Policoff and Jeffrey Skinner. Chicago Review Press.

- Suggestions, advice and activities for young writers. Uses examples of young writers' works.

Teachers and Writers Collaborative
5 Union Square West
New York NY 10003
(212)691-6590

- Catalog of books and materials to assist in teaching beginning and advanced writing skills.

Total Physical Fun: Strategies and Activities for Learning Language Through Cooperative Play
by Jo Ann Olliphant
Sahmarsh Publishing
11004 111th St. SW
Tacoma WA 98498
(206)584-7473

- Games and activities that offer entertaining and effective ways to support your specific teaching goals. Provides step-by-step instructions on how to animate play. More than 100 games and activities.

What's Whole in Whole Language, by Ken Goodman.
Heineman Press.

- Wisdom about how children really learn. Suggestions of ways in which children gain literacy skills. Discusses the methods that either free or constrain them in their efforts.

The Word Detective
by Heather Amery and Colin King
EDC Publishing
8141 E 44th St.
Tulsa OK 74145

- A unique introduction to six parts of speech through the adventures of Inspector Noun. This book is also available in French and German.

The Writing Road to Reading, by Romalda Spalding.

- The following two companies offer programs based on Spalding's phonics book:

The Riggs Institute
4185 SW 102nd Avenue
Beaverton OR 97005
646-9459
Fax: 644-5191

- A traditional, teacher-directed, phonetic approach to teaching reading, writing, and spelling. Riggs offers a taped study course for teachers, phonogram cards, and more.

Spalding Education Foundation
15410 N. 67th Ave., Suite 8
Glendale AZ 85306
(602)486-5881

- Multi-sensory phonics program.

Writing Strands
National Writing Institute
7946 Wright Rd.
Niles MI 49120
(616)684-5375

- Structured writing program designed to teach explanatory, creative, argumentative, and report writing.

Writing Tutor
Louise Tooke
PO Box 3404
Grand Junction CO 81502
(303)464-7626

- Multi-level, ages 8 to 16. Includes essay question aids. 42 lessons on 3 tapes, 75 pages, optional software. $49.95 plus $5.00 shipping. Sample lessons, $3.50.

Reference Books

The following resources are excellent aids for parents. You might also check out the reference/parents' shelf in the children's section of your local library. I have found some surprisingly useful treasures there.

Children and Books, by Zena Sutherland. Scott, Foresman. Glenview, Illinois, 1981.

- More than you would ever want to know about children's literature - very thorough. Written for university level children's literature classes.

Guiding Gifted Readers, by J. Halsted. Ohio Psychology Publishing. Columbus, Ohio. 1988.

- Gifted children have different reading styles and needs. If you have a gifted child, this is a good resource. Covers preschool through high school age people.

Parent's Guide to Children's Reading, by N. Larrick. Westminster Press, Philadelphia, 1982.

- Good suggestions of types and variety of books available for enjoyable reading.

Read-Aloud Handbook, by J. Trelease. Penguin Books, NY 1985.

- Tips on reading aloud. Over half of the book is a list of suggested books the author has read aloud, from picture books to novels. Includes commentary.

Reading Resource Book, by M. Jett-Simpson. Humanics Limited, Atlanta, Georgia, 1986.

- Very good general parent guide, but this book does consider the school to be the child's primary teacher. Has good pointers never the less and includes suggested readings.

Reading, Writing, and Caring, by O. Cochrane. Whole Language Consultants, Winnipeg, Manitoba. 1985.

- Technical, but well written and worth reading.

Writing Because We Love To: Homeschoolers at Work, by Susannah Sheffer
Holt Associates
2269 Massachusetts Ave.
Cambridge MA 02140

- The editor of GWS, Susannah Sheffer, worked through the mail with homeschooled writers ages 10 to 15. Includes samples of kids' work and issues that affect the writing of self-directed learners.

Writing on Both Sides of the Brain, by Henriette Anne Klauser.
Harper Row: 1986

- If parents have writing blocks left over from their school training, this book may help. Klauser's light-hearted style and candor can help you rediscover that writing can be fun and break up your mental blocks for good. Teens may benefit from this book as well.

Writing to Learn, by William Zinsser, also author of *On Writing Well*.
Harper Row: 1988

- Zinsser, in the process of telling us how to write—and think
  —clearly about any subject at all, demonstrates the thesis
  that "to write is to learn." He discusses how he learned and
  wrote about subjects across the curriculum including: math,
  art, music, physics, chemistry, nature, and more. Appropriate for teens or for adults who want to improve their writing
  and thinking skills, or anyone who wants to enjoy some fine
  writing.

Wishes, Lies, and Dreams: Teaching Children to Write Poetry, by
Kenneth Koch. Vintage Books Chelsea House Publishers, 1970

- Excellent resource for writing poetry.

CHAPTER 18
Children's Periodicals

Children love to get something in the mail, and an interesting magazine is no exception. Science, history, social studies, geography, literature, consumerism - you name it, there is a magazine for kids on most topics of interest. With the possible exception of math, an entire curriculum could be created by mail! What better way to introduce new and timely topics to your children? If they discover a lifelong interest in the process, hooray! If not, they will develop general knowledge in many areas.

The magazines listed here are for many ages and interests. You may be able to find some of them at your public library. Children's Magazine Guide, a subject index to many children's magazines, is another useful resource that your library may have.

Be sure to consider subscribing to those magazines and newsletters written by young people as well. A listing of publications by and for children is found in Chapter 19.

3-2-1 Contact
PO Box 53051
Boulder CO 80322-3051

- Magazine of science and technology. Published by the Children's Television Workshop. $15.97/12 issues/year.

American Girl
PO Box 420210
Palm Coast FL32142-9896
(800)845-6005

- A magazine for everyone who owns an American Girl doll and other children interested in the history of women. $19.95/six issues per year.

Boomerang!
123 Townsend Street, Suite 636
Sand Francisco CA 97107
(800)333-7858

- A monthly children's audio magazine, presented on 70 minute tapes and designed for a 7-12 year old audience. A free sample: $2 (shipping and handling.) Trial subscription (3): $12.95. Yearly subscription: $39.95 for 12 issues.

Boy's Life
1325 W. Walnut Hill Lane
PO Box 152079
Irving TX 75015-2079

- Published by Boy Scouts of America. $15.60/12 issues per year.

Calliope: World History for Young People
30 Grove Street
Peterborough NH 03458

- Ages 8 to 14. $17.95/5 issues per year.

Chickadee
255 Great Arrow Ave.
Buffalo NY 14201-3082

- For younger siblings of readers of *OWL*. Published by The Young Naturalist Foundation. $14.95/10 issues per year.

Child Life
PO Box 7133
Red Oak IA 51591-0133
(800)274-4004

- A health oriented, general interest magazine combining fitness and ecology features, activities, children's contributions, and more. Ages 7 to 9. $13.95/8 issues per year.

Cobblestone
30 Grove St.
Peterborough NH 03458
(603)924-7209

- The history magazine for children. Ages 8 to 14. $22.95/10 issues year.

Cricket
PO Box 52961
Boulder CO 80322-2961
(800)284-7257

- Many lovely stories and activities for children. $29.97/12 issues per year.

Faces: The Magazine about People
30 Grove St.
Peterborough NH 03458
(603)924-7209

- A magazine about people and customs published in cooperation with the American Museum of Natural History, New York. Ages 8 to 14. $21.95/9 issues per year.

Hidden Pictures
PO Box 53781
Boulder CO 80322-3781

- Puzzles and activities with emphasis on hidden pictures. Published by *Highlights*.

Highlights for Children
PO Box 269
Columbus OH 43219-0269
(300)255-9517

- "Fun with a purpose." A school style magazine emphasizing basic skills, creativity, and activities. Ages 2 to 12. $21.95/11 issues per year.

Hopscotch: The Magazine for Girls
PO Box 164
Bluffton OH 45817

- Focuses on activities that appeal to girls, without glitzy commercialism. Includes book reviews, and readers can share through poems and letters. Ages 7 to 10. $13.50/6 issues per year.

The Horn Book Magazine
14 Beacon St.
Boston MA 02108

- A magazine about books for children and young adults. Appropriate for young adults and adults interested in literature, book writing, and authors. $36.00/6 issues year.

Jack & Jill
Box 10003
Des Moines IA 50340

- Elementary stories and activities. $11.95/8 issues per year.

Kid City
PO Box 53349
Boulder CO 80322

- For graduates of *Sesame Street Magazine*. $13.97/12 issues per year.

Kids Discover
170 Fifth Avenue
New York NY 10010
(800)284-8276

- Focuses on topics such as pyramids, the North and South Poles. Well-planned and informative. Ages 6 to 12. $14.95/10 issues per year.

Ladybug
PO Box 58343
Boulder CO 80321-83443
(800)284-7257 ext. 212

- A magazine for pre-school or early elementary aged children by the publishers of *Cricket*. Large print designed for early readers. $29.97/12 issues per year.

National Geographic World
Department 00991
17th & M Streets, N.W.
Washington DC 20036

- A magazine published for junior members of the National Geographic Society — a mini version of the big one. Ages 8 to 14. $12.95/12 issues per year.

Odyssey
21027 Crossroads Circle
PO Box 1612
Waukesha WI 53187-1612

- Space exploration and astronomy for young people. $21.00/12 issues per year.

Otterwise: For Kids Who Love Animals
PO Box 1374-Dept. N
Portland ME 04104

- ". . . humane education is the most effective way to change people's attitudes and prejudices toward all living things." Ages 8 to 13. $8.00/4 issues per year.

Owl
255 Great Arrow Ave.
Buffalo NY 14207-3082

- A discovery magazine for children. Published by The Young Naturalist Foundation. $14.95/10 issues per year.

Planet Three: Earth-Based Magazine for Kids
PO Box 52
Montgomery VT 05470
(802)326-4669

- Informative and activity-rich magazine with a strong ecology message. Ages 7 to 12. $14.00/5 issues per year.

Provoking Thoughts
I.D.E.A., Inc., Institute for the Development of Educational Alternatives
PO Box 1004
Austin MN 55912
(800)828-1231

- A "bimonthly magazine devoted to the thinker in all of us." Brain teasers and activities designed to stimulate each of the different types of intelligence as defined by Howard Gardner in *Frames of Mind*. Best if parent and child do these activities together.

Ranger Rick
8925 Leesburg Pike
Vienna VA 22184-0001

- Wildlife magazine for elementary age children. Incredible photographs. Published by the National Wildlife Federation. Ages 6 to 12. $15.00/12 issues per year.

Sesame Street Magazine
PO Box 55518
Boulder CO 80322-5518

- Activities and stories Sesame Street style. $14.97/12 issues per year.

Skipping Stones: A Multicultural Children's Quarterly Forum
PO Box 3939
Eugene OR 97403-0939

- Articles are rewarding and informative for people of all ages. $15/4 issues per year. Reduced rates for Third World and low income subscribers.

Sports Illustrated For Kids
PO Box 830609
Birmingham AL 35283-0609

- A junior version of *Sports Illustrated*. Published by TIME, Inc. $15.95/12 issues per year.

Your Big Backyard
8925 Leesburg Pike
Vienna VA 22184-0001

- A preschool wildlife magazine full of wonderful photographs. Published by the National Wildlife Federation.

Zillions
PO Box 3760
Jefferson City MO 65102

- A consumer reports magazine for children that reviews current fads, and informs kids about advertising methods designed to entice them to buy. A good buy for a child who is fascinated with consumer fads. Ages 8 to 14. $16.00/6 issues per year.

Zoobooks
PO Box 85271
San Diego CA 92138
(800)334-3302

Published by Wildlife Education, *Zoobooks* highlights a different animal each month. Past issues include parrots, birds of prey, night animals, the cheetah, butterflies, gorillas, rhinos, etc. $15.95/10 issues per year.

Reading is to the mind,
what exercise is to the body.
—JOSEPH ADDISON

CHAPTER 19

Children Writing To And For Children

Publications By Children

More and more homeschooled young people are discovering the fun of publishing, writing for, and reading their own publications. Desktop publishing makes it all so easy! This section includes publications which are published and written entirely by kids, as well as some that are published by adults and edited and/or written by young people.

Don't be discouraged if some of the newsletters listed here are no longer published when you contact them — the kid publishers may have moved on to other projects. If it is a newsletter you were especially interested in, why not try publishing a similar newsletter yourself? State and national homeschooling magazines will announce your project, and you can take it from there!

Hey! Check This Out!
Haypenny Press
211 New St.
West Patterson NJ 07424

- A magazine by and for kids to "encourage reading, writing, creativity and independent thought."

Children's Express Quarterly
30 Cooper Square
New York NY 10003

- Age 10 and up. A fifteen page magazine with the appearance of an adult publication. Includes articles on national and international issues that interest young people, such as divorce, gangs, and more. Write for a complimentary copy.

The Gold Mine
Celeste Chan
6101 Ravenna Ave. NE
Seattle WA 98115

- A homeschooling magazine for kids with special sections that include pen-pals, art, dance, and free ads. One year subscription is $6 or 20-21 $.29 stamps. A six month subscription is $4 or 14 $.29 stamps.

The Homeschoolers' Historical Network
Lluvia Crockett
1820 County Rd. 616
Walsenburg CO 81089

- A network of homeschoolers age 10 and over who write articles about any person or event in history that interests them. $10 per year/6 issues.

Home-Schooled Kid
Maggie Cole
96 Acorn St.
Millis MA 02054

- Newsletter for kids ages 3-8, consisting entirely of writings (stories, letters, poems, interviews, etc.) by young homeschoolers. $16 per year/6 issues. Sample issue $3.00.

It's Kids!
Jennifer Richman
3490 Beaver Ford Rd.
Woodbridge VA 22192

- A bi-monthly magazine designed for kids and produced by kids ages four to twelve. Subscribers are encouraged to submit short stories, poems, art work, reviews, and other items. Subscriptions are $10/year. Sample issue is $2.

Kids Works Quarterly
Timothy Morris
6405 NE Cleveland Avenue
Portland OR 97211-2403
289-2586

- Includes articles, stories, poems, black and white drawings, comic strips, and jokes. Send a SASE for sample copy. $3.50/4 issues per year.

Kids Writing to Kids
Kristin and Andrea Horlings
1513 Tara Court
Forest Grove OR 97116

- Your ideas, stories, poems, and artwork are welcome. Subscription cost is $3 for four issues.

Merlyn's Pen
98 Main St.
East Greenwich RI 02816

- A national magazine for student writing. $14.95/4 issues year.

New Moon: The Magazine for Girls and Their Dreams
424 Lakeview Ave.
Duluth MN 55812
(218)728-5507

- "New Moon provides a workplace where girls and women create a magazine which celebrates girls, explores the potential and magic of the passage from girl to woman, and encourages resilience and healthy resistance to the social and cultural inequities girls experience because of their gender." Looking for many kinds of material from girls aged 8-14. Send for information and writers' guidelines. Sample issue/$5.

The Niche
7950 N. Seward Ave.
Portland OR 97217
(503)283-0864

- "The Bi-Weekly High School Open Forum of Free Expression" welcomes contributions from high school age youth (14 to 18) from anywhere on Planet Earth. The point of the publication is "to allow high school students of every ability to see their writing in print." The editors are eager to include contributions, both writing and artwork (pen and black ink), from homeschoolers. Writers guidelines are included in each issue. Subscriptions are available outside the Portland area, and you are free to photocopy. (Free copies are available in Portland at several libraries.) Advertising is welcome. Write for a free sample copy. A terrific local resource!

On the Write Track
Meghann O'Day
255 Caney Creek Rd
Conway AR 72032

- A young writers' magazine that is just in the planning stages. Will carry fiction, non-fiction, poetry, and opinion pieces by older kids. Write for information.

One Earth Trading Post
HC 60 Box 81E
Points WV 25437

- Leenie Hobbie's family's newsletter, which "promotes creative simplicity as a viable alternative to consumerismand a sueful ally for families." Articles about things you can make yourself, living simply. $10/6 issues. Free sample.

Peace on Earth
Colin King
RR #2 - Maple Hill, Box 178A
Long Prairie MN 56347

- An environmental newsletter published by a homeschooler. Looking for articles written by kids. $3/year.

Platypus Egg
Meghann O'Day
255 Caney Creek Rd
Conway AR 72032

- A young writers' magazine that is just in the planning stages. Will carry fiction and poetry of younger kids. Write for information.

Quaere Verum
PO Box 23
Rayne LA 70578

- Edited by Mary Bercier, a homeschooling teenager. Focuses on issues pertinent to teens. Written mostly by kids, and a few parents. Free, four times a year.

Self-Schooler's Network News
RR 1 Box 452
Lisbon Falls ME 04252

- Published by homeschooling teenagers Zoe Blowen-Ledoux and Elizabeth Farsaci. ". . . poems, book reviews, short stories, etc. It does have a peaceful/liberal attitude and we also print articles on other topics submitted and suggested by our readers loosely associated with topics of that bias." $3/four issues.

Spotlight
Joshua Beidler
PO Box 304
La Quinta CA 92253

- *A* newsletter about the environment, published by and for kids. Subscriptions are $3 per year.

Stone Soup
PO Box 83
Santa Cruz CA 95063

- This classic magazine contains only children's work. Stories, poems, book reviews, and art of children through age 13. $23/5 issues per year.

To Kids For Kids By Kids Newsletter
11,119 Pucket Pl.
Midlothian VA 23112

- A newsletter for homeschooling children edited by homeschooler Sherri Raynor. They currently have over 200 subscribers. Subscriptions are $4/year.

Total Baseball Cards Monthly and two teen newsletters
Josh White
10201 Adams Rd.
Galena OH 43021

- Issues are 18-22 pages long, full of art by homeschoolers, graphics, and stuffed with helpful articles, player profiles, and investment tips. Aimed at the 12-18+ age range. $18/year or $9/6 mo. Sample issue/$1.50.

- Josh is starting two new newsletters for teens. One includes inspirational writing for Christian homeschoolers, and the other is for quality high school and college level writing. Free for the postage.

The Young and the Literate
Melyssa and Laryssa Landrum
1304 Third St.
Baker City OR 97814

- Published monthly at $.75 per issue or $6.60 per year. Submissions and subscriptions are always appreciated. Poems, stories (including installment stories), recipes, art, and more.

❖

Pen Pal Resources

Have you heard about the homeschooled student who has fifty pen pals from around the world? (Read about this young woman in Grace Llewellyn's book Real Lives*) She is getting a terrific education!*
    Even the most reluctant writer has a hard time ignoring letters from pen pals. Children who are too young to write meaningful letters might send audio tapes, photos, drawings, stickers, stamps, etc., to pen pals, until writing skill develops.
    Here are some sources for finding pen pals that you might try. Pen pal listings are often included regular children's magazines (See Chapter 18.)

Growing Without Schooling
2269 Mass. Ave.
Cambridge MA 02140

- Lists names, ages, and interests of homeschoolers looking for pen pals.

Home Education Magazine
PO Box 1083
Tonasket WA 98855

- Lists names, ages, and interests of homeschoolers looking for pen pals.

Kidcare Communications
117 West 95th St., Suite 2F
New York NY 10025-6635
(800)851-9001
Contact: Serena Mendiola

- An organization to help kids develop pen pal contacts in other countries.

Oregon Home Education Network
4470 SW Hall Blvd., #286
Beaverton OR 97005
321-5166

- Lists names, ages, and interests of homeschoolers looking for pen pals.

Pen-Pal Newsletter
Jennifer Eichholz
228 Waverly Rd.
Wilmington DE 19803-3135

- Send in your name, birthdate, address, and a letter describing yourself and your interests. Articles on hobbies, birthday twins, and more. Send a SASE for subscription information.

US Postal Service Olympic Pen Pal Club
PO Box 9419
Gaithersburg MD 20898-9419
(800)552-3922

- The club matches members ages 6 to 18 in the U.S. with their peers in 14 foreign countries. Club members receive a kit filled with materials for letter-writing, a coloring book, a world map. $5.95 per member.

CHAPTER 20

Math

Think of math as a language that describes the world we live in. Early mathematics exposure occurs best in a child's natural habitat — counting, measuring, estimating, dividing, sharing, cooking, building, taking apart, always questioning the world in his natural way. The use of hands-on math materials is recommended as a way to easily bridge the way from the natural world to abstract math concepts. Some favorites are listed below, and Chapter 15, Instructional Materials Catalogs, has additional resources.

I am a firm believer in using games for skills practice. For example, the game Yahtzee provides practice with multiplication facts through six, and addition with carrying. The whole family can play, because younger kids can calculate their scores using Cuisenaire rods or counting collections. Cribbage (and many other card games), dominoes, Monopoly, and Scrabble are just a few games that provide calculation practice. Computers and calculators can also provide enjoyable and useful drill and practice.

This section includes suggested math manipulatives, books, programs, catalogs, and centers.

Abacus

- The ancient Asian calculator. Useful at many levels of math skill, from counting through multiplication and division. Good for learning place value.

Algebra the Easy Way, by Douglas Downing. Barron's Educational Series.

- Covers the topics of high school algebra via an adventure story.

Anchor Math: The Brain-Compatible Approach to Learning Math, by Leslie A. Hart. Books for Educators, PO Box 20525, Village of Oak Creek AZ 96341. (602)284-2389.

- An informal book for all who teach elementary math and want to greatly increase student achievement. Homeschoolers who want to avoid workbook burnout will enjoy this book.

Marilyn Burns Education Associates
150 Gate 5 Road, Suite 101
Sausalito CA 94965
(405)332-4181

- Burns' books are excellent. They encourage a creative application of mathematics to the real world. Find as many as you can. Try *Math and Literature (K-3), About Teaching Mathematics, A Collection ofr Math Lessons, The I Hate Mathematics Book, Math for Smarty Pants, Math for Girls*, more.

Chisanbop Books

The Complete Book of Fingermath, by Edwin M. Lieberthal. McGraw-Hill Book Co., 1979.
and
Chisanbop, Chisanbop Enterprises Inc., PO Box 99, Mt. Vernon, New York, 10551.

- Chisanbop is a system of counting to ninety-nine using your very own ten fingers. A terrific exposure to place value and counting in base five. Uses the same principle as the Chinese abacus. The two books are by the same author and are essentially the same.

Counting Collections

- Use what you have, or create a special new collection just for math practice. Try stones, shells, beads, coins, keys, game pieces, toy cars, or what-have-you. How about leaves, garden produce, foods, and other perishables?

Cuisenaire Rods
Cuisenaire Co. of America
12 Church St., Box D
New Rochelle NY 10805
(800)237-3142, (914)235-0900, FAX (914)576-3480

- Excellent manipulative math materials. Also publishes a math and science catalog. Useful for teaching mathematical concepts including multiplication, division, fractions, and algebra. Many useful peripheral materials, including workbooks and instruction materials, are available.

Family Math, by Tenmark, Thompson & Cosey

- Excellent math resource, includes various activities for a variety of academic abilities.

Games for Math: Playful ways to help your child learn math from K to grade 3, by Peggy Kaye.

Get It Together: Math Problems for Groups Grades 4-12, from Equals, Lawrence Hall of Science, UC-Berkeley.

- A superb collection of "cooperative logic" problems that are best solved in groups. I have used problems from this book successfully with a group of mixed-age homeschoolers. Beautifully constructed problems that challenge, yet require the participation of all members of the group. Can be used with individuals. Many math concepts are covered.

Gotcha and *Aha!*, by Martin Gardner.

- Fascinating puzzles and problems for the more advanced math student.

Hands-On Equations Learning System
Borenson and Associates
PO Box 3328
Allentown PA 18106
(215)820-5575

- A confidence-building introduction to algebra using manipulatives, designed for children eight years old and up.

Hands-On Learning
417 Haines Avenue
Fairbanks AK 99701
(907)456-8356
1-800-770-MATH

- Quality math manipulatives, problem solving activities, games, puzzles, and books of thought-provoking activities.

Lane County Mathematics Project
Dale Seymour Publications
PO Box10888
Palo Alto CA94303

- An unusually useful math series that focuses on problem solving. Grades 4-8 plus Algebra. Check your library.

Lennes Math Essentials of Arithmetic
Child's Way Inc.
37895 Row River Rd.
Culp Creek OR 97427

- 4th-9th grade math program stressing practical application through word problems.

Math Learning Center
MLC Materials
PO Box 3226
Salem OR 97302
370-8130

- The Center "promotes . . .strategies that emphasize sensory perception, visual reasoning, mathematical discourse and appropriate assessment." Excellent resource for visual math materials and programs. Catalog. Geoboards, fraction materials, pattern blocks, books, and more. Good prices.

Math In the Mind's Eye, by Bennett, Maier, and Nelson
Math Learning Center
PO Box 3226
Salem OR 97302

- An extended program of visual hands-on learning activities for grades 4-12. Very useful approach for students who think that math is the manipulation of pencil marks on paper, or who have been burned by school math.

Maths in the Mind, by Ann and Johnny Baker
Heinemann Educational Books, Inc.
361 Hanover St.
Portsmouth NH 03801

- Builds on children's natural learning styles and unique understanding of math processes.

Math Their Way, by Mary Baratta-Lorton
Center For Innovation in Education, Inc.
19225 Vineyard Lane
Saratoga CA

- Manipulative K-2 hands-on program used by many progressive schools. Also *Mathematics: A Way of Thinking*. Grade 3-4 program. Workshops are offered to help teachers learn to use the program.

Math Products Plus
PO Box 64
San Carlos CA 94070
(415)593-2839

- Sixty pages of math manipulatives, math history, math enrichment, math entertainment, instructional math books; puzzles and puzzle books; math T-shirts, jewelry, posters; much more.

A Mathematical Mystery Tour: Higher-Thinking Math Tasks, by Mark Wahl.

- Approaches math as a way of looking at the world. Many projects and puzzles.

Mathematics: A Human Endeavor, by Harold Jacobs.

- Addresses the spirit and beauty of math as well as computation skills. Enjoyable math book for high school and up.

Mindstorms, by Seymour Papert.

- Discusses LOGO, the children's programming language, and its use in the creative teaching of math and logic.

Mortensen Math
(800)338-9939

- Call for free catalog. Manipulative mathematics with grade level manuals. Materials are available for basic skills (counting, matching, etc.) through algebra and calculus.

"Provoking Thoughts"
Institute for the Development of Educational Alternatives
PO Box 1004
Austin MN 55912
(800)828-1231

- A "bi-monthly magazine devoted to the thinker in all of us." Includes math puzzlers and problems. Card style format so that activities can be clipped and filed.

Saxon Math Books
1320 W. Lindsey
Norman OK 73069
(405)329-7071

- Straightforward math texts, for children who are really ready for abstract math concepts and who thrive on practice. New concepts are introduced in every lesson, and are reviewed and built upon through daily practice. From 4th-5th grade through algebra, geometry, and trigonometry and calculus. Saxon books can be purchased from:

  The Children's Book Barn, 4570 SW Watson, Beaverton OR 97005
  641-2276

  Thompson Book Depository, PO Box 60160, Oklahoma City OK 73146
  (405)525-9458, FAX (405)524-5443

  Mustard Seed Education Svs, 120 Winston Section Rd, Winston OR 97496

"Wonderful Ideas"
The Institute for Math Mana
PO Box 64691
Burlington VT 05406

- Sample issue $4.

CHAPTER 21
Science

Science begins for the very young in the kitchen, the yard, the stream, the beach, and the sky. Homeschoolers can build on natural interests by focusing on hands on activities and experiments. The best science books are the ones with lots of activities in them. The OMSI Store in Portland (Chapter 26) is a good source of quality science books and materials. Investigate the children's periodicals section (Chapter 18) for some excellent science magazines. See also the general instructional materials catalogs in Chapter 15.

Instructional Books and Resources

Aves Science Kit Co.
PO Box 229
Peru ME 04290
(207)562-7033

- Supplies traditional biology and chemistry programs and units at a reasonable cost for grades 8-12.

Backyard Scientist
PO Box 16966
Irvine CA 92713

- Hands-on science experiments in physics, chemistry and the life sciences. Four books to choose from. SASE for free brochure.

"Clearing - environmental education in the pacific northwest"
Creative Educational Networks
Environmental Education Project
John Inskeep Environmental Learning Center
19600 S. Molalla Ave.
Oregon City OR 97045
24 Hour Environmental Education Hotline (800)322-3326

- A newsletter of ideas, activities and resources for teaching about the environment.

The Earth Guys
731 W. 26th St.
Houston TX 77098
(800)868-6588 (orders)
(713)868-1827 (The Guys)

- Quality hands-on science and nature toys and activities, including both old favorites and interesting new items.

The Exploratorium Snackbook
Exploratorium Publications
3601 Lyon Blvd.
San Francisco CA 94123
(800)359-9899

- Nothing to eat here, just "Teacher created versions of Exploratorium Exhibits." 107 hands-on science projects, each a simple, inexpensive version of an Exploratorium exhibit or demonstration. Sample projects include building an electroscope, a fog chamber, a gas model, pan pipes, an electric motor, and a vortex tube.

Eyewitness Books

- Many titles covering specific areas such as fossils, shells, etc. Wonderful photographs. Available at many bookstores.

Hands On Nature; Information and Activities for Exploring the Environment with Children
Vermont Institute of Natural Science
Woodstock VT 05091
(802)457-2779

- Nature book for exploring your environment first-hand.

Hidden Stories in Plants, by Anne Pellowski

- Stories from all over the world that have been told in association with common plants. Many plant activities are included. Combines science and literature.

Insect Lore Products
The Science and Nature Company
P.O. Box 1535
Shafter CA 93263
(805)746-6047
Orders: (800)LIVE BUG

- Catalog with lots of nature related items.

David Macaulay Books

- This author has written many enjoyable books, including *The Way Things Work* and *Castle*. Try to find them all if you can.

Science and Children; NSTA Reports
Published by the National Science Teachers Association
1742 Connecticut Ave. NW
Washington DC 20009
(202)328-5200

- Lists about 300 free science resources per year; available to members.

Science Experiments You Can Eat and *More Science Experiments You Can Eat.* By Vicki Cobb

- Two fun science books using kitchen items - you can eat the results.

Science Through Children's Literature
by Carol M. Butzow and John W. Butzow.
Delta Education, Inc.
PO Box 950
Hudson NH 03051
(800)442-5444

- An unusual early elementary science program, using children's literature as a springboard for many interesting activities.

The Scientist Within You: Experiments and Biographies of Distinguished Women in Science, by Mary H. Thompson and Rebecca Lowe Warren. ACI Publishing, PO Box 40398, Eugene OR 97404.

- Women's achievements in science and math from the first century A.D. to the present. Kitchen table type experiments.

Scotts Valley Books
PO Box 67241
Scotts Valley CA 95067
(800)508-5484
On-Line Book Search: (408)336-0248 (1200 or 2400 bps, n, 8, 1)

- Science and nature. Homeschoolers can take 15% off prices.

Sharing Nature With Children: The Classic Parent's and Teachers' Nature Awareness Guidebook and *Sharing the Joy of Nature; Nature Activities for All Ages.* By Joseph Cornell.

- Two enjoyable nature books.

Teaching Science to Children, an Integrated Approach, by Alfred E. Friedl.

- If you can only buy one science book that will last for a long time, this one will guide you through many science explorations. Includes scientific explanations of each event.

Tops Learning Systems
10970 S. Mulino Rd.
Canby OR 97013

- Science task cards related to a specific area in science i.e. pendulums, metric measure, light, electricity, machines, etc.

Usborne Books. Many titles to choose from. Many pictures and detailed facts. Non-traditional format.

World of Science Division
1665 Buffalo Road
Rochester NY 14624
(716)426-1450

- Catalog available for $2.00.

❖

Science Equipment And Suppliers

American Science and Surplus
601 Linden Pl
Evanston IL 60202
(708)475-8440

- Incredible stuff, unbelievable prices. Sixty-three pages of items in categories such as optical, electrical, mechanical, teaching aids, bearings, military, plumbing, and much more. Items are carefully described so that you know what you are getting. You won't know how badly you really need this stuff until you start reading the catalog.

Edmund Scientific Company
101 E. Gloucester Pike
Barrington NJ 08007-4397
(800)533-4397

- Not an educational science supplier, but a fascinating source of real science and technical materials.

Nasco Science Catalog
901 Janesville Ave.
Ft. Atkinson WI 53538
(800)558-9595

- Huge catalog of science materials.

The important thing is not to stop questioning . . .
Never lose a holy curiosity.
—ALBERT EINSTEIN

CHAPTER 22

Social Studies

The social studies section creates a small dilemma. Social studies (history, geography, civics, economics, cultural studies, and so on) can easily become dry and boring when separated from the richness of the world around us. An easy way to kill children's interest in social studies is to require them to complete structured social studies courses and materials, regardless of interest.

On the other hand, the best way to develop a lifelong love of history and geography, and people's interactions with one another, is to follow the child's interests and needs.

Is she interested in trains? Immerse yourselves in trains. Go to train stations and museums; read train books; learn how trains were developed and how the transcontinental railroad was built; ride on trains; build model trains; meet some engineers, conductors, and brakemen; count train cars; calculate freight weight or boxcar volume; and so on. How have trains changed the ways people live? How did the Intercontinental railroad influence the West? How are trains different in other countries? What art and music can you find that relates to trains? Save up to take a train trip and see the country.

Virtually any topic of interest has a history. That history can be developed into a springboard to acquiring more general knowledge of the past as well. Scour the resource and catalog sections of this book and other homeschooling magazines and books for ideas that fit your particular child's interests. It may take a while, but eventually you will happen on to a topic that excites your child. You'll notice, after getting involved in the study of an interest, that you have covered many other "school subjects" along the way. Congratulations! You have an "integrated curriculum," the elusive goal of many modern schools! Or call it unit studies if you prefer. You may want to focus all of your history studies around activities until your children are old enough to want to read to find out more.

History and other social studies materials, texts, and resources are widely available. History and geography magazines for both children and adults are plentiful. Most of the catalogs in the catalog section of this book offer many social studies materials. Browse through a few to see what they have to offer.

Following is a list of generic materials, resources, and suggestions for your social studies program, and two wholehearted recommendations for catalogs that have particularly rich offerings.

The Basics

There are a few basic materials and resources that should be available to all children as they grow up and learn about the world.

- A globe

- A world atlas, or access to many maps

- An encyclopedia set (a used garage sale set may be good enough)

- A time line (home made or purchased)

- Trips to local historical sites and museums (Chapter 26)

- Frequent use of the local library

- Selected videos, computer programs, and television programming

- Selected magazines (Chapter 18)

❖

Enrichment

These extras should be included regularly, as time, interest, and resources allow.

- Biographies

- Historical fiction

- Cultural, historical, and geographical nonfiction (not textbooks)

- Artifacts (such as ancient coins, arrow heads, cultural items from another country or another time, ethnic dress, etc.)

- Materials for fantasy play and exploration of another culture, such as dress up clothes, paper dolls, coloring books

- Models and model-making materials

- Role playing activities (such as: churn butter, write with quill pens, read by candle light, make soap, learn dances, games, and songs of the time or place, re-enact battles or historical events, etc.)

- Selected computer programs, videos, and public television programming

- Historical board games

- Geography puzzles and games

- Participation in local music, art, dance, sports, ethnic, and cultural activities

- Family vacations and trips that take in local culture, history, and geography

- Road maps and aeronautical and navigation charts

- Selected textbooks as references

Resources

Bluestocking Press
PO Box 1014
Placerville CA 95667-1014

- American history and government resource. Materials in this catalog are carefully selected to be consistent with the principles of America's Founders. This means a historian is reporting history "standing on the shoulders of Jefferson." That is probably a good guideline for choosing American history materials. *Bluestocking* contains everything you will ever want related to Laura Ingalls Wilder and her books. Miscellaneous materials such as games, art books, cookbooks, tapes, map placemats, toys, and activity books are included, and there is a smattering of materials on other subjects besides history. Jane Williams (a homeschooling parent herself) has a selection of quality materials that you can rely on.

Hands On History
201 Constance Drive
New Lenox IL 60451

- This company is run by two homeschooling moms who believe in "immersion learning" is the best way to teach history. They offer Immersion Kits, which are collections of items for children to use as they "experience" history through their play. Three large kits are available: Columbus, Revolutionary Boy, and Revolutionary Girl. Many other items are available. While you can certainly put together your own items for immersion studies, you might find these materials to be a quicker and easier alternative.

CHAPTER 23

Art

A variety of good art supplies, together with art books and prints from your local library, can go a long way toward a successful art program. You might try seeking instruction from a local artist or some art classes in your community. In addition, many useful art materials can be found in the general catalog section. Visit local art galleries. Art museums are an excellent resource for art prints and art history materials. Look for craft books and craft projects at your local craft store. Those who want to provide a little extra at home may find the offerings below useful

A. G. Petunia Artworks
5605 Keystone Pl. N.
Seattle WA 98103
(206)632-7464

- Catalog of art supplies.

Annie B's Home School Art Supplies
481 South 2nd
Cornelius OR 97113

- Quality supplies available by mail. Send SASE for information.

Art Education Resources
Crystal Productions
Box 2159
Glenview IL 60025
(800)255-8629; Fax(708)657-8149

- Catalog of art prints, technical (including mask making instruction), portfolio prints, art timelines, videos, books, and games. More than 2000 items - good resource for the serious student of art.

ART-i-FACTS
PO Box 67192
Topeka KS 66667

- A monthly newsletter offering art history with related activities, craft and seasonal activities, and tips for adults who wish to offer creative art experiences to children. A useful tool for "not-so-artsy" parents who want to give their kids a quality art experience at home. Subscription $12.00 per year.

Creative Art for the Developing Child, by Clare Cherry. David S. Lake Publishers.

- Varied approaches of doing art with young children. Developmental and process oriented. Lots of ideas.

Creative Kids Club
PO Box 60
Mill Valley CA 94942
(415)388-4138

- Art activity kits that include materials and instructions. Holiday Card Kits for eight different holidays, Calendar, Greeting Cards, Party Invitations, and Make Your Own Book.

Draw-A-Long & Create
Creative Children's Connection
2330 Ragan Woods
Toledo OH 43614
(419)865-6131

- An art instruction package that includes a video instruction tape, instruction manual, charcoal pencils and kneaded erasers. $29.95 plus $5 shipping.

Drawing on the Right Side of the Brain, by Betty Edwards

- A course in enhancing creativity and artistic confidence. This book claims it can teach you to draw even if you feel you have little talent.

Drawing With Children, by Mona Brookes. St. Martin's Press.

- A creative method of teaching and learning drawing that can be used even if you have little art experience of your own. You learn along with your children.

Hearthsong Catalog
2211 Blucher Valley Rd.
Sebastopol CA 95472

- Many craft kits, ranging from basketry and weaving to dream-catchers and candlemaking.

Kids Art News
Kidsart
PO Box 274
Mt. Shasta CA 96067

- Quarterly fine arts activity newsletter for kids.

Kids Multicultural Art Book, by Clare Cherry. Williamson Publishing.

- Art projects from around the world. Short explanations of cultural significance. Uses many found and recycled supplies.

Painting With Children, by Brunhild Muller. Floris Books.

- Waldorf book on painting with young children.

Step By Step Series, by Deri and Jim Robins.
Kingfisher Books
Grisewood & Dempsey Inc.
New York NY 10016

- Includes *Collage, Making Prints, Making Kites*, and *Papier-Mache*. Clear instructions and illustrations.

❖ ❖ ❖

The family is one of nature's masterpieces.
—GEORGE SANTAYANA

CHAPTER 24

Music

Music is learned in two ways: by listening to it and by performing it. Singing to and with young children and listening to records and tapes that you both enjoy may be all the music you need for a long time. Add in some fun with rhythm instruments (homemade or purchased), marching and dancing, and a more terrific music program cannot be found. Old classroom music books can be a good resource. **Classical Kids** compact discs and tapes are popular.

If you need further resources, many of the general homeschooling catalogs offer a good selection of music items. **John Holt's Book and Music Store** and **Music for Little People** are favorites.

As the child matures, singing in a local homeschool, church, or community choir or learning to play an instrument may give him a lifelong love and appreciation of music. Some children like to learn to play recorders together, others enjoy traditional piano or violin lessons, and still others like to play around with a synthesizer for hours on end. Forcing music on a child can be worse than no music program at all, so be sure to follow your child's interests as much as possible.

.   Homeschooled students can participate in public school music activities, such as orchestra and band, if the school participates in interscholastic music activities. See Appendix A for the exact wording of the law and rules regarding interscholastic participation.

(An excellent songbook you may want to look for is: *Rise Up Singing: The Group Singing Songbook*, edited by Peter Blood and Annie Peterson, and published by Sing Out Corp., PO Box 5253, Bethlehem PA 18015-0253. This songbook includes words, chords, and sources of 1200 songs, from ballads to Beatles, Bob Dylan to Broadway.)

Music is the universal language
of mankind.
—Henry Wadsworth Longfellow

CHAPTER 25

Physical Education And Health

Physical Eucation is the easiest subject of all to incorporate into the homeschool program because children so naturally love to move and to try new physical skills.

If your child has been "burned" by a bad school PE program, take your time in helping that child get involved in physical activities, and be sure that you don' call it PE. If your child naturally shies away from daring or competitive activities, there are many quieter things to do, such as hiking, swimming, weight lifting, bicycling, or dancing.

Try physical activities that family members can enjoy together. Homeschoolers often try many different things over the years. One family's list includes swimming, dancing, gymnastics, softball, basketball, tennis, canoeing, trampoline, running, hiking, horsebackriding, skating, yoga, skiing, archery, and tree climbing.

If your older homeschool student wants to participate in competitive sports, your local park and recreation district may offer the activities you want. Your neighborhood school may have an after-school program in which you can participate.

Interscholastic sports and activities offered by the public schools are available to all homeschooled students. Read Appendix A for the exact wording of the Interscholastic Participation portion of the law, and Chapter 2 for an interpretation.

Health and nutrition are best learned through normal family activity. If you are looking for specific material, try the instructional materials catalogs and textbook suppliers listed in Chapters 15 and 16, a health store, book store, or your family health care provider.

True enjoyment comes from
activity of the mind and exercise of the body;
the two are ever united.
--HUMBOLDT

CHAPTER 26

Local Community Learning Resources

Some of the best learning opportunities are to be found right at our doorsteps. Museums, historical sites, living history pageants, career learning opportunities, and more, are just waiting to be explored.

Write to the Visitor's Center or Chamber of Commerce in the communitythat you plan to visit, for a packet of information. Local businesses and industries are often very willing to be visited.

Most places that offer field trips to public schools will schedule a field trip for homeschoolers if you ask. Remind your children to be respectful of the rules and guidelines, and to show your gratitude (a handwritten thank you note or a drawing is always appreciated) to the tour guide for his or her time and effort. You can teach your children appropriate public behavior, and at the same time pave the way for other homeschoolers to be welcomed as well.

This listing is just a sampling of what you can find. The majority of these resources are in or near the Portland metropolitan area, central Oregon, and the North Coast. I am sharply aware of how many other wonders of Oregon I have yet to discover.

If your favorite resources have not been included here, why not share them with other homeschoolers via a statewide newsletter?

Be sure to call ahead. Details such as open times and fees are subject to change without notice.

Thanks to Jan Hunt for sharing her favorite Bend area resources; and to Ranell Curl for help with Eugene area resources and many state resources.

❖

Central Oregon-Bend Area

Places To Go

Dee Wright Observatory
33.7 Mi. via Hwy. 126, 242
Redmond

- 1/2 mi. paved self-guided loop over lava beds.

High Desert Museum
South Highway 97
382-3408

- Natural history museum: classes, nature trails, native plants, otters, and porcupines. 9-5 daily. High Desert Museum Nature Store has natural and cultural history items, educational learning tools. Museum admission is not required to visit the store.

Lava Butte/Lava Lands Visitor Center
593-2421

- An extinct volcanic cone with three trails, and a paved road to the top. The Visitor Center offers automated displays, slide shows, and related gift items. Naturalist on duty. 9-4 daily, Mid-March through October.

Petersen Rock Garden
10 miles N. of Bend, off Hwy. 97

- Open daily 8 am - dusk. One hour. Adults $1.50, 6-16, $.50.

Pine Mt. Observatory
25 Mi. E. of Bend
382-8331

- Call first. Public encouraged after April on Fri. and Sat. evenings. Suggested donation, adults $2.00

Redmond Air Center
1740 SE Ochoco Way
Redmond
548-5071

- Smoke jumper facility. Tours M-F, 8-4. Groups call ahead.

Reindeer Ranch
2.2 mi. via Hwy 126 from Redmond

- More than 100 reindeer and Arabian horses.

Sunriver Nature Center
593-1221, ext. 394

- Local natural history exhibits, nature trail, botanical garden, public programs. Raptor counting expedition in late winter. Summer classes for children. Professional staff. A small store specializing in field guides. 10-12 Tue., 10-4 Wed.-Sat., closed Sun. and Mon.

U.S. Forest Service Silviculture Laboratory
1027 NW Trenton

- Headquarters for field study of timber growth and lab. for investigating ecological factors. Visitors welcome. 7:30-4 pm Mon.-Fri. Free.

Central Oregon Retail Resources

The Book Barn
124 NW Minnesota

* Friendly and fast special orders; children's library; discount for regular customers.

The Curiosity Shoppe
140 NW Minnesota
382-3408

* Only outlet for *Mothering* magazine.

Natural Resource Center
1005 NW Newport
385-6908

* Small but unique and interesting selection of nature/science books, toys, recycled paper products, and environmental information. Non-profit; staffed by volunteers; hours may vary.

Eugene/Springfield

Places To Go

Dorris Ranch
South 2nd St. and Dorris Ave.
Springfield
726-4335

* Living History Farm. Call ahead for a schedule of events. Adults $2, under 18 $ .50.

E.W.E.B.
500 E. 4th
Eugene
484-2411 Ext. 401, Evan Gentry

* Water filtration tour, near Weyerhauser; Main Plant tour; Leaburg Dam & Fish Hatchery; Nature hike at Leaburg Dam. Will also talk on electrical safety, conservation, or other topics.

Hult Center
7th and Willamette
Eugene
687-5087

* Oct. - May. Free noon concert on Thursdays, followed by a tour at 1 pm.

Mt. Piscah Arboretum
34901 Frank Parrish Rd.
Eugene
747-3817

* Spring flowers in May. Call in Jan. for May group tours. Self-guided tours available.

Telephone Museum
113 E. 10th
Eugene

* Tue. and Thu. 10-2 pm.

University of Oregon
13th and Agate
Eugene
346-4195

* General campus tour, or call a department for a specific tour.

University of Oregon Theatre
Eugene
346-4195

- Janet Rose. Tour to see backstage, prop room, costuming.

North Coast Resources

Places To Go

The Astoria Column
From Marine Drive, turn onto 16th Street and follow the signs
Astoria

- Built in 1926, this 125 foot high observation platform offers, on a clear day, a 360-degree view of the mouth of the Columbia, the Astoria Bridge, the Pacific Ocean, 4 smaller rivers, four towns, three bays, and several mountains. Open 7:30 am to nightfall. Free, for the 166 step climb.

Fort Astoria
Exchange and 15th
Astoria

- Located one block west of the Heritage Center, this is a partial reconstruction of Fort Astoria, the first white settlement west of the Mississippi River. Free.

Fort Clatsop National Memorial
South of Astoria, off Highway 101
861-2471

- A historically accurate reproduction of Lewis and Clark winter quarters built on the site in 1805-06. New visitor's center. Living history programs and more are offered in the summer months. Open 8 am to 5 pm daily, 8am to 6 pm from Father's Day to Labor Day. $1 admission 17-61, all others free, maximum charge is $3 per family.

Fort Canby
off Highway 101, 2 miles SW of
Ilwaco WA
(206)642-3078

- Lewis and Clark Interpretive Center, built high on a cliff . Park open 7:30am to dusk daily through September. Camping sites available by mail reservation only: PO Box 488, Ilwaco WA 98624. Interpretive Center open daily from 9 am to 5 pm through September. Free.

Fort Columbia
off Highway 101, one mile west of the Astoria Bridge
Chinook WA
(206)777-8221
(206)777-8358

- Original buildings of the Coast Artillery Corps forts. Interpretive center is open 9 am to 5 pm daily from mid-May through mid-September, and by appointment only for the rest of the year. Free. Excellent place for panoramic views of the Columbia River, hiking and picnicking. Park hours 6:30 am to dusk throughout the summer.

Fort Stevens State Park Historical Interpretive Center
Warrenton

• Oregon's largest state park. Great bicycling and camping. Daily living history exhibit with a working blacksmith shop. Interpretive Center is open May 1 to Labor Day, 10 am to 6 pm. Underground tour, $2.

Jewell Wildlife Management Area
State Highway 202, 27 miles SE of Astoria
From Highway 26, take Hwy. 202, east of Elsie

• This refuge for several hundred Roosevelt elk is operated by the Oregon Department of Fish and Wildlife and is the only one of its kind in the state. Viewing areas just off the highway.

Museums

Camp 18 Logging Museum
18 miles east of Seaside on Highway 26
755-2476

• An outdoor museum of antique logging equipment, including an old steam crane, two train cabooses, and a steam donkey. Open daily, 7 am to 9 pm, free.

Clatsop County Historical Society
1618 Exchange St.
Astoria
325-2203

• Operates the three museums listed below. Admission to all three museums in $5 for adults and $2.50 for children 6 through 12. Any two museums, $4 for adults, and $2 for children.

Astoria Firefighters' Museum
2968 Marine Drive
Astoria

• A new museum housed in a former fire hall. The collection contains antique firefighting gear, some dating back to the 1880s. Open Friday, Saturday, and Sunday from 10 am to 5 pm.

Flavel House Museum
441 Eighth Street
Astoria

• Elegant Victorian mansion that was built in 1885 by Captain George Flavel, master of a sailing fleet. Distinguished by a fourth story cupola used by the captain and his wife to watch river traffic. Open daily from 10 am to 5 pm through September.

The Heritage Museum
1618 Exchange St.
Astoria

• Regional artifacts, traveling exhibits and an art gallery, housed in the restored 83-year-old former Astoria City Hall. 10 am to 5 pm daily through September.

Columbia River Maritime Museum
1792 Marine Drive
Astoria
325-2323

• Nationally acclaimed museum. Many boats and models, including the Columbia Lightship No. 604, and a full-size reconstruction of a sailing gillnet fishing boat. Rope-making demonstrations from 1 pm to 4 pm most Fri., Sat., and Sun. Open daily 9:30 am to 5 pm.

Ilwaco Heritage Museum
115 SE Lake St.
Ilwaco WA
(206)642-3446

- This museum is devoted to the history of the Long Beach Peninsula area. Open Monday through Saturday, 9 am to 5 pm, and Sunday from 12 noon to 5 pm, year-round. Admission is $1.25 for adults, children under 12, $.50, senior citizens, $1.

Seaside Museum and Historical Society
570 Necanicum Drive
Seaside
738-7065

- Recently reorganized and re-opened with new displays. Open daily, year-round, from 10:30 am to 4:30 pm. Admission is $2 for adults, $1.50 for seniors, $1 for youth ages 13-17, children under 12 free.

Tillamook County Pioneer Museum
2106 Second St.
Tillamook
842-4553

- Exhibits include shipwreck artifacts, blacksmith tools, natural history, Victorian relics, blacksmith tools, logging, a stagecoach and old cars. Open Mon.- Sat. during the summer, 8:30- 5 pm, and Sun. 12- 5 pm. Admission is $1 adults, $.50 for students 12 to 17, $5 for families, and children under 12 free.

Portland Metro Area Resources

Roughly defined, the northern Willamette region is anywhere you can get to and back in a day trip to or from the Portland metro area. Some SW Washington resources are included.

Places To Go, Things To Do

Bird Haven
41795 Kingston Lyons Drive
Stayton OR 97383
769-5597

- Observe local bird living patterns, view bat roosts, and enjoy organic gardens. A private organization that provides an educational demonstration area showing the advantages of working with the natural order of nature. Open March till August. Call ahead.

Chrysalis
Concord Choir, Inc.
PO Box 2636
Portland OR 97208
760-3722

- A community choir for youth ages 9 to 14. An opportunity for choral singing and training. Call or write for more information.

Jackson Bottom Wetlands
123 W. Main St.
Hillsboro OR 97123
681-6205

- 3000 acre wildlife sanctuary, interpretive trail. Bird watch checklist, educational materials available for loan.

Lelooska Foundation
165 Merwin Village Road
Ariel WA 98603
(206)225-9522

- Kwakuitl tribe program featuring authentic dances, masks, and story-telling around a blazing fire in the center of a long house. Presented by the Lelooska family. Evening adult-oriented program or school group day program. Call or write for reservations in early spring.

Pacific Northwest Live Steamers
Shady Dell Park
31083 S. Shady Dell Ave.
Molalla
829-6866

- Free rides on a miniature steam locomotive. May-Oct., Sun., 9-6.

Pomeroy Living History Farm
20902 NE Lucia Falls Road
Yacolt WA 98675
(206)686-3537

- An educational museum that depicts 1920's farm life in the pre-electrical era. Costumed interpreters take part in many farm activities. Offers school programs, private group hay rides, and A.S.L. Interpretation. "Theme" Teas.

Portland Bureau of Parks and Recreation
1120 S.W. 5th Room 1302
Portland OR 97204-1976
796-5193

- Many classes offered from gymnastics, to drawing, to skiing, at more than reasonable prices. Guide to activities available at neighborhood centers.

Saturday Academy
19600 N.W. Von Neumann Dr.
Beaverton OR 97006-1999
690-1190

- Non-profit organization offering classes after school and on Saturday for kids "grades" 6 - 12. Classes taught by professionals. Tuition charged, scholarships offered. Architecture, chemistry, engineering, animals, astronomy etc.

Tualatin Hills Park and Recreation District
15707 SW Walker Road
Beaverton OR 97006
645-6433

- Similar to Portland Bureau of Parks and Recreation. Pick up a schedule of activities from any District Pool, the Rec Center. Very reasonable prices.

Tears of Joy Theatre
1109 East Fifth Street
Vancouver WA 98661
(206)695-3050

- World class puppet performances. Offers a summer puppetry camp. Sponsors the International Children's Festival.

Museums

The American Advertising Museum
9 NW Second Ave.
Portland OR
226-0000

* Wed.-Fri. 11am-5pm. $3 adults, $1.50 seniors, children 6-12 years.

Children's Museum - Clay Workshop
3037 SW 2nd
Portland OR
823-2227

* Tues.-Sat. 11am-5pm, Mon 9am-1pm. $3 adults, $2.50 children, Mon. free. Open format for clay exploration. You can purchase a bag of clay so you can take home your creations. Clay classes also offered. Clay shop is open every Wed. from 9:30 - 4:30. Free with Admission $3.00 adults $2.50 kids. Mon. is family day. (9:30 - 1:00)   Call ahead.

Cowboys Then & Now Museum
729 NE Oregon Street
Portland OR 97322
731-3333

* Wed.-Fri., 11am-5pm; Sat. and Sun., noon-5pm. Free admission. The evolution of the American cowboy and the cattle industry. A one hundred year old, fully-equipped chuck wagon; photo murals; Wild West Show posters; barbed wire; a library; Western art; interactive exhibits; more.

Hart's Reptile World
11264 S. Macksburg Rd.
Canby OR
266-7236

* Over 300 reptiles on display. Age 7 and up, $3; 3-6, $2; 2 and under free.

Georgia-Pacific Historical Museum
900 SW 5th Avenue.
Portland
222-5561, ext. 7981

* Tours by appointment. Open Tue.-Fri., 10-3 pm.

Jeff Morris Memorial Fire Museum
SW Front at SW Ankeny
Portland OR
823-3700

* Walk by every day. Free.

Kidd's Toy Museum
1300 SE Grand Ave.
Portland OR
233-7807

* Displays between 7000 and 8000 American-made toys manufactured as early as the 1870's and as late as the 1940's. Mon.-Fri., 8am-5:30pm; Sat., 8am-1pm. Free. Tours can be arranged.

Maryhill Museum of Art
35 Maryhill Museum Dr.
Goldendale WA
773-3733

* Interesting museum includes Rodin art, native American exhibits, chess sets, more. Picnic area; pescocks. Stonehenge replica nearby. Hours: 9 am-5 pm every day. $4/adults, $1.50/ages 6-16, $3.50 seniors, under 5 free.

Oregon Art Institute, Pacific Northwest College of Art
1219 SW Park
Portland OR
226-2811

• Many quality classes for children and young adults. Spendy, but scholarships offered. Tues.-Sat. 11-5pm, Sun. 1-5pm, Mon. closed. $3 adults, $1.50 students, $.50 Children 6-12 years. Members free, seniors (62 and up) free on Thursdays. First Thursdays free 4pm- 9pm.

Oregon Historical Society
1230 SW Park
Portland OR
222-1741

• Mon.-Sat. 10am-5 pm, Sun. 12-5 pm. Great history resource and bookstore.

Oregon Jewish Museum
292-6474

• One of Portland's newest museums; does not yet have a facility. Call for time and place of next exhibit.

Oregon Maritime Museum
113 SW Front
Portland OR
224-7724

• Winter: Fri., Sat., Sun., 11am-4pm. Summer: Wed.-Sun., 11am-4pm. $2 adults, $1.25 students, seniors, $4.50 family. Members and children free.

Oregon Military Museum
Camp Withycombe
Clackamas OR
657-6806

• Fri. and Sat. 1pm-5pm, other times by appointment. Admission free.

OMSI (Oregon Museum of Science and Industry)
1945 SE Water Ave.
Portland OR 97202
797-4000

• 9:30 am-5:30 pm, Sat.-Wed., 9:30 am-9 pm Thurs. and Fri. $6.50 adults, $4.00 students (3-17 years). $5.50 seniors (62 and up), members free. Exhibits, classes, & physics, chemistry and computer labs. Ask about a homeschoolers class age 12 and older.

Stark's Vacuum Cleaner Museum
107 NE Grand
Portland OR
234-9325

• Mon., Fri. 8am-8pm. Tues.-Thurs. 8am-6pm. Sat. 9am-6pm, Sun. closed. Admission free.

State of Oregon Sports Hall of Fame and Museum
Standard Insurance Center
900 SW Fourth
Portland OR
227-7466

• Mon.-Sat. 10am-3pm. Admission free.

Trails and Heritage Center
211 Tumwater
Oregon City OR
655-5574

- Mon.-Fri. 10am-5pm. Sat., Sun.
  1pm-5pm. $3 adults, $2 seniors,
  $1.50 children 6-12 years, $7.50
  family of 5 or more.

Washington County Museum
17677 NW Springville Road
Portland OR
645-5353

- Mon.-Sat. 9am-4:30pm. $1
  adults, $.50 ages 6-17, under 6
  free, $3.00 families.

Willamette Falls Ship Locks
At the falls on the Willamette River
West Linn
656-3381

- National historic site. Operated
  daily 7-11 pm. Tours M-F
  11am-2:30. Call in advance. Then
  cross the river to Oregon City and
  ride the public elevator "vertical
  street" up the cliff.

World Forestry Center
4033 SW Canyon Road
Portland OR
228-1367

- Every day 10am-5pm. $3 adults,
  $2 students (6-18 years). Seniors
  (62 and up), members and under
  6 free.

Metro Retail Resources

Audubon Society Bookstore
5151 NW Cornell Road
Portland OR
292-6855

Book Barn for Children
4570 SW Watson
Beaverton OR 97005
641-2276

- Quality children's books. They
  want to work with homeschoolers, and offer a 15% discount to
  homeschoolers, except on Saxon
  math books.

Child's Play
907 NW 23rd
Portland OR 97210
224-5586

Children's Books - Gresham
79 NW Miller Ave.
Gresham OR 97201
661-5887

Children's Place
1631 NE Broadway
Portland OR 97232
284-8294

- Excellent selection of children's
  books

Country Tales Ltd.
229 E. Main
Hillsboro OR 97123
693-9838

- Children's books for all ages.

**Ginger & Pickles Bookstore for
Children**
425 Second
Lake Oswego OR 97034
636-5438

Learning Palace,

- Teaching materials and supplies.

  ○ **Canyon Place**
  Beaverton OR 97005
  644-9301

  ○ **Eastport Plaza**
  3972 SE 82nd
  Portland OR 97206
  775-0848

  ○ **Town Fair Center**
  818 NW Eastman Parkway
  Gresham OR
  661-0865

  ○ **Vancouver Store**
  7809 NE Vancouver Plaza
  Vancouver WA
  Portland phone 285-0305

  ○ **Liquidation Center**
  4455 SE 52nd Ave.
  Portland
  775-6097
  Fri. and Sat. 11-5.

Learning Skills
11530 SW 72nd Ave.
Tigard
684-0647

- Home teaching materials and tutoring. Math Haters Program.
  Call for appointment.

Learning World

- Teaching materials, supplies,
  math manipulatives, books, and
  more.

  ○ **Beaverton Mall**
  3155 SW Cedar Hills Blvd.
  Beaverton OR
  643-6538

  ○ **Vancouver**
  13503 SE Mill Plain Blvd.
  Vancouver WA

**Oregon Historical Society
Bookstore**
1200 SW Park Avenue
Portland OR
222-1741

Powell's Books
Powell's Books for Kids
Cascade Plaza, across from
Washington Square
Tigard OR
761-0671

**Printing Office Bookstore - U.S.
Gov't.**
1305 SW 1st
Portland OR
221-6217

School Daze
Tigard Plaza
11945 SW Pacific Hwy.
Tigard OR
624-9085

Title Wave Used Books
216 NE Knott
Portland OR
294-3243

- Used books from Multnomah
  County Library.

Other Oregon Communities

Here is a sample of the many learning opportunities to be found in our state. To list all would be to write a different book. Enjoy!

Albany

James River Corporation
30470 American Drive
Albany
369-2293, ext. 232

• Paper production. Tours June-Aug. 9:30 am and 1:30 pm. Large groups call in advance.

Tele Dyne Wah Chang Albany
1600 NE Old Salem Road
Albany

• Metal research. Tours every Fri., 10 am. 13 years and older. Reservations preferred.

U.S. Bureau of Mines
1450 Queen Ave. SW
Albany
967-5816

• Research of reactive metals. Advance notice required for tours.

Ashland

Oregon Shakespearean Festival
Pioneer and Main Streets
482-4331

• Backstage Theatre Tour, 10 am Tue.-Sun. Call in advance.

Baker City

Oregon Trail Interpretive Center
Hwy. 86, 5 mi. E. of Baker City
(800)523-1235

• An outstanding 23,000 square foot exhibit of the Oregon Trail experience, mining, explorers and fur traders, native American history, natural history, and more. Open daily except Christmas and New Years, 9-6, May-Labor Day, 9-4, Labor Day-Apr. 30. Free.

Bandon

Bandon Foods, Inc.
680 E. 2nd
Bandon
347-2456

• Cheese processing plant tour. Mon.-Sat., 8:30-6 pm, Sun. 9-5 pm.

Coos Bay

Coast Guard Boat Station
Boat Basin
888-3266 or 888-3267

• Tours, call ahead.

Corvallis

Benton County Courthouse
120 NW 4th
Corvallis
757-6831

• Guided tours of 1888 courthouse. Call for appointment.

The Dalles

Wonderworks Children's Museum
505 W 9th St.
The Dalles
296-4864

* Hands on, learning by doing, museum. Tue.-Sat., 10-4:30 pm. $1.25 per person.

Muirhead Canning Co.
5267 Mill Creek Road
The Dalles
296-9778

* Fruit cannery. Tours July-Sept. Call ahead.

Grants Pass

Fourply Inc.
124 NE Beacon Drive
479-3301

* Plywood. Call in advance for tours.

Myrtlewood Products Inc.
1785 Dowell Road
479-6664

* Myrtlewood factory. Tours 9-4:30 pm all year.

Hood River

Diamond Fruit Growers
Chevron Drive
Hood River
386-3111

* Fruit nursery. Call in advance for tour, Sept.-Feb. 7-3:30 pm.

Juanita's Tortilla Factory
2885 Van Horn Drive
386-6311

* Food manufacturer. Call in advance for tours.

Luhr Jensen & Sons Inc.
400 Portway
Hood River
386-3811

* Fishing lures and equipment. Call in advance.

John Day

John Day Fossil Beds
Hwy. 26, NW of John Day
575-0721

* Fossil exhibits from the Age of Mammals. M-F, 8-4:30 pm year around.

Joseph

Boise Cascade
Hurricane Creek Highway
432-2011

* Sawmill. Call in advance. Tours Tuesday only.

Eagle Mountain Gallery
307 W. Alder
432-0325

* Bronze foundry. Call ahead. Tours daily. $3.00 fee.

Klamath Falls

Carriage Works
707 S. 5th
Klamath Falls
882-0700

* Horse-drawn carriages.

MDA/PDC Inc.
1120 Spring St.
882-2594

- Computer parts manufacturer.
  Call in advance.

Oregon Institute of Technology
882-6321

- Geo-heat center. Call for
  appointment.

La Grande

Boise Cascade
1917 Jackson Street
La Grande
962-2000

- Lumber products. Tours. Call
  ahead.

Fleetwood Travel Trailers
Pierce Lane & Hwy 22
963-7101

- Trailer manufacturers. Tours. Call
  ahead.

Lebanon

Linn Gear Corporation
100 N. 8th Street
Lebanon
259-1211

- Gear manufacturing. Call ahead.

Lincoln City

Lacey's Dollhouse and Museum
3400 NE Hwy. 101
Lincoln City
994-2392

- Mor than 2000 dolls; coins, old
  guns, and musical instruments.
  Open daily 8-5 pm.

Medford

Harry & Davids
Jackson & Perkins
2836 S. Pacifiic Highway
776-2277

- Fruit products and rose gardens.
  Tours. Call in advance.

Medford Corporation
N. Pacific Highway
773-7491

- Plywood mill. Tours, self-guided.
  7:30 am and 2:30 pm.

Southern Oregon Agricultural
Experiment Station
569 Hanley Rd.
772-5165

- Agricultural experiments. Tours
  year around, M-F, 8-4 pm. Call
  ahead.

Monmouth

Hollister-Stier
3395 S. Pacific Highway
838-2315

- Pharmaceutical raw materials.
  Tours May-Sept. 8-2:30 pm.

Newport

**Mark O. Hatfield Marine Science
Center**
2030 S. Marine Science Drive
Newport 97635
867-0100

- OSU's Marine reasearch and education facility. Public aquarium
  and information center open daily
  10-4 and 10-6 during the summer. Educational programs are
  offered to groups..

Oregon Coast Aquarium
2820 SE Ferry Slip Rd.
PO Box 2000
Newport 97365
867-3474

- Located on Yaquina Bay. Offers hands on educational programs for K-8 students. Send for details. Regular hours are Winter, 10-4 pm, Mon.-Sun. and Summer, 9-6 pm, Mon.-Sun.

Oakridge

Gold Lake Park (Snow Park)
off Highway 58 at the top of the pass.

- Cross country skiing, trails for all abilities. Buy parking pass at Sportsman's Cafe.

Willamette Fish Hatchery
76389 Fish Hatchery Rd.
782-2933

- Fish hatchery tours.

Pendleton

Hamley & Co.
30 SE Court
Pendleton
276-2321

- Saddle making and rope tying. Tour. Call ahead.

Pendleton Woolen Mills
1307 SE Court Place
276-6911

- Woolen processing plant. Tours at 9, 11, 1:30, and 3 pm, M-F.

Port Orford

Knutsons Handcrafted Clocks
530 West 8th
Port Orford
332-1905

- Clock manufacturer. Tours Mon.-Sat., 9-4 pm. Call in advance.

Roseburg

Oregon Romney Wool
3885 Melqua
673-7913

- Harriet Cornachione. Hand processing wool. Call in advance for tours.

Roseburg Forest Products Co.
Old Highway 99S
Roseburg
679-3311

- Tours; call in advance. Ten years and older.

Sunrise Enterprises, Inc.
1950 NW Hulholland Drive
Roseburg
673-0195

- Products and services by handicapped persons. Tours; call in advance.

Salem

Baskett Slough Refuge
12 miles west of Salem, off Highway 22

- 2,492 acres.

Gilbert House Children's Museum
116 Marion St. NE
Salem OR 97301-3437
371-3631

- Closed Mon. $2/person, under 1 free. Groups of 10 special rates with a reservation. The Water Room; Inventor's Workshop; Outer Space Theater; Kidspace; A Walk in the Woods; Children Around the World.

Llamaland
20 miles south of Salem
769-7297

- Second largest llama ranch in U.S. Call for tour reservation.

Mission Mill Museum
1313 Mill St. SE
Salem
585-7012

- Restored woolen mill; mission houses; Tues.-Sat., 10-4:30. Summer, Sun. 1-4:30; Marion Museum of History, picnicking, shops.

State Capitol
Salem
378-4423

- Tours of the tower every 1/2 hour. 9-9:30 M-F, 9-4 Sat., 12-4 Sun. Ask to see the Supreme Court.

Western Baptist College Archaeology Museum
5000 Deer Park Drive
Salem
581-8600

- Pre-Columbian artifacts; Middle Eastern artifacts.

Farm Equipment and Truck Museums
3995 Brookdale Rd. NE
Brooks
393-2424

- Antique power land. Caretaker can open buildings if closed.

Sweethome

Custom Services Inc.
2210 Tamarack
Sweethome
367-2121

- Planing mill and kiln. Call in advance. Twelve years and up.

South Santiam Tree Farm
367-5168

- Ranger Station.

Umatilla

McNary Lock and Dam
922-3211

- Hydro-electric power plant. Tours June-Sept. Call ahead.

Vale-Burns-Lakeview

Southeast Oregon Auto Tour
Harney County Visitor Information
18 West "D" Street
Burns 97720
573-2636

- Lake, Harney, and Malheur counties include almost 1/4 of Oregon real estate. Hart Mt., Steens Mt., Malheur Cave and Lake, Glass Buttes, Diamond Craters, Fort Rock, Crack in the Ground, hot springs, rockhounding, bird watching, pronghorn antelope.

❖

Useful Publications

The Oregonian, or your local newspaper; The Phone Book; literature from Visitors' Centers and the local Chamber of Commerce.

- The best and most current information about your community resources. Many learning activities can be built from and with these common publications. These "obvious" resources may be overlooked. Here is a gentle reminder.

Around Portland With Kids, by Judi Siewert & Kathryn Weit
Discovery Press
PO Box 12241
Portland OR 97212

- A book filled with lots of good ideas, but call ahead.

Discover Seattle with Kids
by Rosanne Cohn
JASI Discover Books
PO Box 19786
Seattle WA 98109
(206) 454-7333

- Same as above, for Seattle.

Encouraging Words Field Trips and Newsletter
Susan Buck
9783 Broadacres Rd. NE
Hubbard OR 97032

- A unique resource. Susan has done her homework, and knows tons about field trips and resources. Your support group might want to subscribe to this resource. A Christian resource, open to all.

Eugene Days: Places to Go With Children in the Eugene -Springfield Area, by Jan Gilmore and Carol Nielsen.

- Extensive field trip resources.

Going Places, and *Family Getaways in the Pacific Northwest*, by Ann Bergman

- Places to go in Washington, Oregon, and British Columbia. Includes hotels, dude ranches, bed and breakfasts, town events, museums, attractions, restaurants, things to do on the road, and how to get there.

Kids Yellow Pages, by Lois Shenker & Barbara Vanselow

- A kids directory from "Amusement Places" to "Zoos".

MAGEN (Metro Area Gifted
Education Network)
Multnomah ESD
11611 NE Ainsworth Circle
Portland OR 97230-9039
(503) 257-1628

- Newsletter of resources and
  information related to gifted
  children, their teachers, and
  parents. Subscriptions free to
  Multnomah County residents,
  $10/yr./$2 issue for others.

*Museums in Oregon Pocket
Guide*
Oregon Museums Association,
c/o OHS
1230 SW Park
Portland OR 97205

- A brochure listing most of the
  museums in Oregon, including a locator map of Oregon,
  open times, and key exhibits.

Portland Family Calendar
600 NW 14th
Portland OR 97209

- Calendar of Kid and Parent
  activities published monthly.
  Free around town or get 12 issues for $12.

Portland Kids
White Publications
PO Box 952
Lake Oswego OR 97034

- Includes outings, tours, restaurants, clothing, resale, bookstores, skating rinks, pools,
  dance instruction, birthday en-
  tertainers, theater, more.

Portland Parent
Northwest Parent Publishing
PO Box 19864
Portland OR 97223
(503) 245-8036

- Monthly news magazine for
  parents . Publishes an Education Directory that includes a
  homeschool resource listing.
  Free around town or $12/yr
  subscription.

The Portland Walkbook, by
Peggy Robinson
Far West Book Service
3515 NE Hassalo
Portland OR 97232

- Lists local walks with dis-
  tances, time, directions, description, and map.

Part Four

Religious Resources

Three world religions (Islam, Christianity, and Judaism) are represented in these chapters. Materials and resources have been found suitable to homeschoolers from each faith. The collections are not intended to include all resources, but to get you started, and to give you an idea of what is available.

If you seek homeschooling resources for other religions, contact religious leaders. Any materials used in religious education programs are probably adaptable to your homeschooling situation. You might want to contact an inclusive statewide or national homeschooling organization from time to time to see if materials have become available since the publication of this handbook.

Those who deny freedom to others
deserve it not for themselves, and, under a just God,
cannot long retain it.
--ABRAHAM LINCOLN

CHAPTER 27

Christian Resources

The materials, organizations, and resources include all that may be classified as having a Christian perspective. Those programs having a particular perspective (i.e., Mennonite, Catholic, fundamentalist, Seventh Day Adventist, etc.) are indicated when known. If you have questions about the content of any program, ask before you buy. Most support groups will be happy to help you identify what you are looking for. Many of the organizations listed are willing to work with anyone, regardless of faith.

My thanks to Ranell Curl of LIGHT *and Sue Welch of* The Teaching Home *for their kind help in rounding out this section.*

State, Local, and Regional Organizations And Groups

Many Christian groups are not listed here. Most of them can be contacted through HIS Net, OCEAN or LIGHT, below.

HIS Net of Oregon (Homeschool Information and Service Network Of Oregon)
PO Box 20985
Salem OR 97303
(503) 699-9241

- Statewide non-profit corporation providing practical assistance to homeschool support groups and individual homeschool families. Board of directors is non-denominational Christian and representative of the five United States Congressional districts. HIS Net serves all homeschoolers regardless of religion or educational philosophy. Bi-monthly newsletter, *The Messenger*, contains articles on opportunities for homeschool students, ideas for support group activities, political information, statewide calendar of events, etc. (Free sample issue upon request.) Newcomer, Support Group Leader, and High School informational booklets due for release in 1995. Support group incorporation and liability insurance information. Computerized telephone referral service for all homeschool support groups.

Holy Rosary Catholic Homeschool Group
(503)698-4992

- Primarily Catholic group in Portland area, but open to all.

Lane Inter-Christian Guild of Home Teachers (LIGHT)
31579 Gowdyville Rd.
Cottage Grove OR 97424
(503)942-0586

- A county-wide Christian network of twelve support groups. Monthly meetings. Sponsors an annual Curriculum Fair each spring,featuring nationally known speakers, workshops, and a used curriculum sale. Publishes a directory of Oregon homeschool support groups and the Oregon Calendar of Events. Open to all.

LDS Contact in Oregon

- Cathy Shauklas, (503)639-2958

Oregon Christian Education Association Network (OCEAN)
2515 NE 37th Ave.
Portland OR 97212
(503)288-1285

- OCEAN is an incorporated non-profit support network for leaders of Fundamentalist Christian homeschool groups throughout Oregon. Connects Fundamentalist Christian homeschoolers with groups anywhere in the state. Fundamentalist Christian events are usually announced on the phone line.

Parents' Education Association (PEA)
PO Box 1482
Beaverton OR 97075
(503)452-1428

- Oregon Christian homeschool advocacy group. Includes a political action committee (PEA PAC) and offers a legislative information hot-line through OCEAN's phone line - (503) 288-1285. Fundamentalist.

Southern Oregon Curriculum Fair

- Write for information. Spring. Sponsored in alternate years by **Jackson County (Christian) Home Educators**, PO Box 295, Talent OR 97540 and **T.E.A.C.H. (Total Education At Christian Homes)**, PO Box 82, Grants Pass OR 97526.

Westside Counties Associated Christian Homeschoolers (Westside COACH)
Membership: (503)699-9241.

- Washington county area support group. Monthly field trips and moms' meetings. Monthly newsletter. Membership requires signed statement of faith, dues, and volunteer work in the organization.

❖

National Organizations and Periodicals

Catholic Home School Newsletter
688 11th Ave. NW
New Brighton MN 55112

The Cheerful Cherub
Box 262302-H
San Diego CA 92196

- Magazine and catalog for homeschooling Catholic families. Sample issue, $2. Six issues/$12.

Christian Life Workshops
PO Box 2250
Gresham OR 97030
667-3942

- Featuring Gregg Harris, a popular advocate of and speaker on fundamentalist Christian homeschooling.

Homeschool Digest
PO Box 575
Winona Lake IN 46590

- Quarterly publication; fundamentalist articles on family life and homeschooling. Written primarily by fathers.

Home School Legal Defense Association (HSLDA)
PO Box 159
Peaonian Springs VA 22129
(703)882-3838

- Prepaid legal defense and assistance— "homeschool insurance"—for those who use a traditional curriculum package and are in full compliance with the law. Associated with NCHE, below.

Homeschooling Today: Practical Help for Christian Families
PO Box 1425
Melrose FL 32666

- National magazine—broad spectrum of Christian standards. Many ideas in each issue, including art, unit stud ies, preschool, teen activities, and more. Reviewed in Chapter 10.

Latter-day Saint Home Educators Association
A Call to Closeness
2770 South 1000 West
Perry UT 84302
(801)723-5355

- Quarterly newsletter for LDS homeschooling families. Four issues/$8. Catalog of resources especially for LDS families is available for $1.

National Association of Catholic Home Educators
PO Box 4202225
San Diego CA 92142

National Center for Home Education
PO Box 159
Peaonian Springs VA 22129
(313) 632-5208

- Associated with HSLDA, above. Helps state leaders monitor legislative concerns and public policy developments.

National Home Education Research Institute
Brian D. Ray, President
Western Baptist College
5000 Deer Park Dr. SE
Salem OR 97301
(206)283-3650

- Conducts and publishes research on homeschooling.

The Parents' Review
PO Box 2910
Eugene OR 97402

- Quarterly magazine for Christian home training and culture following the Charlotte Mason approach.

Practical Homeschooling
Home Life
PO Box 1250
Fenton MO 63026-1850

- Quarterly magazine on the practical aspects of family life and homeschooling from a Christian perspective. Mary Pride, editor. Reviewed in Chapter 10.

Rutherford Institute
PO Box 7482
Charlottesville VA 22906
(804) 978-3888

- Nationwide legal defense organization offering legal services, often without charge, concerning religious constitutional issues.

The Teaching Home
PO Box 20219
Portland OR 97220-0219
253-9633

- Comprehensive national fundamentalist Christian homeschooling magazine; includes an insert from OCEAN, "The Oregon Update." Sue Welch, editor. Reviewed in Chapter 10.

Curriculums, Diploma Programs, Planning Services, And Correspondence Schools

Oregon Based

Basic Educational Consultants
5291 14th Pl. S
Salem OR 97306
585-9088

- Oregon resource for Accelerated Christian Education (ACE) materials K-12.

Basic Skills Assessment Service
19144-B S. Molalla Avenue
Oregon City OR 97045

- Offers testing, a winter workshop and curriculum fair, and other services to the Christian homeschooling community. Fundamentalist.

Child's Way
37895 Row River Rd.
Culp Creek OR 97427

- Offers transcripts, resource library, curriculum counseling, and parent/teacher support.

Cornerstone Family Educators
Linda Reinmiller
3619 SE Caruthers
Portland OR 97214

- Materials for the Moore method and unit studies.

Custom Curriculum Company, "Materials for Learning with Joy"
owned by the David Curl family
76504 Poplar Street
Oakridge OR 97463
782-2571

- Services and materials for historic unit studies. Customized curriculums are developed during a one day consultation, Over 5000 titles—books, games, kits, and cassettes—are offered for purchase. Send $2.00 for a catalog. Oregon History unit study guide. Workshops on subjects of interest, especially unit studies. Open Wed. 9-noon. Will work with all.

Encouraging Words Field Trips and Newsletter
Susan Buck
9783 Broadacres Rd. NE
Hubbard OR 97032
981-6227

- Monthly field trips covering all academic subjects each year. Integrated study materials for trips. Monthly newsletter.

Family Learning Services
Dr. and Mrs. Clayton Crymes
1755 Graham Dr.
Eugene OR 97405

- Testing, counseling, transcripts, and diplomas.

Garden Way Christian Academy
201 N. Garden Way
Eugene OR 97401
683-9538

- Testing, transcripts, band, and other classes. High school diploma program. Works with most curriculum choices.

Mustard Seed Educational Services
Molly Jacobsen
120 Winston Section Road
Winston OR 97496
(503)679-3218

- Many educational materials, some used, including hands-on math materials. Write for a catalog. Molly is a qualified tester, offering group testing throughout Oregon and into southern Washington. Individual testing and consultation available in the Roseburg area.

Nationally Based

A Beka Book Publications
Pensacola FL 32523-9160
(800)874-2352

- Correspondence school. Textbooks, educational materials, video programs. Traditional teacher-directed textbook approach. Grade one of computer aided curriculum is ready.

Advanced Training Institute of America
Box 1
Oak Brook IL 60522-3001
(708)323-7073

- Theme centered units. Applications must be completed and approved, and parents must attend training prior to admission to programs or access to materials.

Alpha Omega Publications
PO Box 3153
Tempe AZ 85280
(800)821-4443 Ext. 112

- K-12 curriculum requires teacher input, partially self-instructional. Uses consumable worktexts (textbooks and workbooks combined).

Alta Vista Curriculum
PO Box 55535
Seattle WA 98155
(800)544-1397

- Integrated K-7 curriculum divided into five units: Plants, People in Groups, Earth and Space, People as Individuals, and Animals. Free brochure. $5 for sample lessons.

Bob Jones University Press
Dept. E-22
Greenville SC 29614
(800)845-5731

- Textbooks and curriculum. Homeschool versions of some teacher's editions.

Christ Centered Publications
2101 N. Partin Drive
Niceville FL 32578
(904)678-9621

- Early childhood curriculum.

Christian Liberty Academy Satellite Schools
502 W. Euclid Ave., Dept. G
Arlington Heights IL 60004
(800)348-0899

- Low cost, complete curriculum consists of books, keys, tests, course instructions; diplomas; K, 1-8, 9-12. Discount books for all subject areas.

Christian Light Education
PO Box 1126N
Harrisonburg VA 22801
(703)434-0750

- K-12 curriculum stresses family values. Phone assistance, record keeping, diploma; tests are available. Mennonite.

The Cornerstone Curriculum Projects
2006 Flat Creek Place
Richardson TX 75080
(214)235-5149

- Math, science, art, and music curriculum packages designed to build a Biblical world view.

Covenant Home Curriculum
Stonewood Village
12200 W. Capitol Dr.
Brookfield WI 53045
(414)781-2171

- Curriculum based on Reformed Evangelical view; includes materials from several publishers. Counseling, grading, and record keeping are available.

Design-A-Study
408 Victoria Ave.
Wilmington DE 19804-2124

- Unit study materials for social studies, spelling, and science..

Hewitt Research Foundation
PO Box 9
Washougal WA 98671
(800)348-1750, Fax: (206)835-8697

- Curriculum and programs for grades 1-12, including special needs and high achievers. Counseling and testing. Seventh Day Adventist.

Home Study International
PO Box 4437
Silver Spring MD 20914-4437
(800)782-GROW

- Seventh Day Adventist. Correspondence courses preschool through college.

KONOS
PO Box 1534
Richardson TX 75083
(214)669-8337

- Teacher directed unit studies coordinated around character trait themes. Combines projects and activities with reading and composition assignments. Includes drill.

Living Heritage Academy
PO Box 1438
Lewisville TX 75067
(214)315-1776

- Uses Accelerated Christian Education (ACE) materials, K-12. High school options include college, academic, and vocational prep. Academic advisors available.

McGuffey Academy International
2213 Spur Trail
Grapevine TX 76051

- Curriculum, teacher assistance, report cards, testing. Personalized curriculum design available.

Moore Foundation, Raymond and Dorothy Moore
Box 1
Camas WA 98607
(206)835-2736

- Offers a variety of educational books, curriculum programs and materials. You can participate in the Moore Academy, the Moore Foundation Independent Study Program, or use materials of your own choosing. "The Moore Homeschooling Formula" —a balance of study, work, and service. Publishes reports on homeschooling. (See Chapter 10 for an in-depth review). Seventh Day Adventist. Open to all.

Mott Media
1000 E. Huron
Milford MI 48381
(313)685-8773

- Republished 19th century textbooks form a basic curriculum for K-8. Biographies of famous Christians.

Rod and Staff Publishers, Inc.
Hwy. 172
Crockett KY 41413
(606)522-4348, Fax: (606)522-4896

- Traditional curriculum from Mennonite publisher, includes workbooks with lots of drill and practice.

The Weaver Curriculum
2752 Scarborough
Riverside CA 92503
(714)688-3126

- Study of scripture weaving in basic school subjects.

Subject Areas

Language Arts

Blendo
Primary Source
PO Box 1711
Cambridge MA 02238

- A reading skills game.

English for the Thoughtful Child
Greenleaf Press
1570 Old La Guardo Rd.
Lebanon TN 37087

- Illustrated composition book for elementary grades. Grammar taught by writing.

Family Learning Center
Rt. 2 Box 264
Hawthorne FL 32640

- *Learning Language Arts Through Literature, Wordsmiths,*
  and *The Great Editing Adventure.* Creative, easy-to-use.

Great Books of the Christian Tradition
Terry W. Glaspey
35 Shoal Dr. E.
Vallejo CA 94591
(707)647-2023

- Hundreds of Christian classics listed in chronological order
  with summaries.

Jensen's Grammar and Wordsmiths
1355 Ferry Rd.
Grants Pass OR 97526

- Incremental approach to language arts.

Simply Grammar
PO Box 2910
Eugene OR 97402

- Illustrated primer emphasizing natural thinking ability.
  Aimed at grades 4-8.

Total Language Plus
PO Box 548
Livermore CA 94550
(510) 606-5841

- Complete language courses based on classic literature.

Progeny Press
200 Spring Street
Eau Claire WI 54703-3225
(715)833-5261
Fax: (715)836-0105

- Bible-based study guides for literature.

Teaching Reading At Home
Back Home Industries
PO Box 22495
Milwaukie OR 97222

- Multi-sensory phonics program based on *The Writing Road to Reading.*

Understanding Writing
Bradrick Family Enterprises
PO Box 2240
Port Orchard WA 98366

- Complete K-12 language program.

Math

Activities for Learning
Dept. B, 21161 York Road
Hutchison MN 55350
(612)587-9146

- Program for teaching math concepts with the abacus. Free catalog available.

Algebra Home Study
Professor Weissman's Software
246 Crafton Ave.
Staten Island NY 10314

- Algebra computer program.

Calculadder
Providence Project
PO Box 1760
Wichita KS 67201

- Math skills program emphasizing calculation and speed. $2.50 for a Trial Pack.

Making Math Meaningful
The Cornerstone Curriculum Project
2006 Flat Creek Place
Richardson TX 75080
(214)235-5149

- K-6 "hands-on" program emphasizing reasoning and problem solving. Also Algebra I program.

Math Mouse Games
Home Run Enterprises
12531 Aristocrat Ave.
Garden Grove CA 92641

- Set includes nine games for K-6.

Math Video Tutor
Bly Academy
PO Box 5878
Kingwood TX 7725
(800)648-4574

- Step-by-step video math programs ranging from addition to differential calculus.

Music

Your Musical Friends
Christian Education Music Publishers, Inc.
2285 185th Place
Lansing IL 60438
(708)895-3322

- Music reading workbooks for K-4.

God Made Music and ***Wee Sing Music***
Praise Hymn, Inc.
PO Box 1080
Taylors SC 29687

Science

Good Science K-6 Curriculum and **Discovery Science Modules**
Education for the Real World
3601 42 St.
Lubbock TX 79413
(806)799-0804

- Programs containing both written content and hands-on learning for the study of literal 6-Day Creation.

Master Books
Institute of Creation Research
4730 Barnes Rd.
Colorado Springs CO 80917

- Creation science materials for preschool through high school.

Of Pandas and People, by Percival Davis
Haughton Publishing Co.
PO Box 180218
Dallas TX 75218-9976

- The science of Creation for jr. high and high school students.

Oregon Outdoor School and Science Camp
Jan Manselle
4808 SE Ina Ave.
Milwaukie OR 97267

- Annual event for 3rd-8th grade students.

The Search
Cornerstone Curriculum Project
2006 Flat Creek Place
Richardson TX 75080
(214)235-5149

- "Discovering the principles that govern God's creation through hands-on activities."

Unlocking the Mysteries of Creation
Creation Resource Foundation
PO Box 570
El Dorado CA 95623

- Literal 6-day Creation book interlinking Bible, history, and
science.

Social Studies

Bluestocking Press
PO Box 1014
Placerville CA 95667

- Moral but not biblical materials. Many social studies items;
specializes in *Little House on the Prairie* related items.

Christian History Magazine
465 Gunderson Dr.
Carol Stream IL 60188

- Quarterly magazine with articles on church history.

Creation's Child
PO Box 30004
Corvallis OR 97339
758-3413

- Terrific timelines for history studies.

Greenleaf Press
1570 Old Laguardo Rd.
Lebanon TN 37087
(615)449-1617

- "Twaddle-free" chronological study of history.

A Guide to American Christian Education for the Home and School:
The Principle Approach, by James B. Rose.
American Christian History Institute
Box 648
Palo Cedro CA 96073
(916)547-3535

Mantle Ministries
Little Bear Wheeler
140 Grand Oak Dr.
San Antonio TX 78232

- Cassette, video tapes, and reprinted books emphasizing America's Christian heritage.

General Curriculum Catalogs

Builder Books
Box 529 1-T
Lynnwood WA 98046
(206)778-4526

- Books, tapes, teaching aids, and games.

Christian Family Resources
PO Box 213
Kit Carson CO 80825-0213
(719)962-3228

- Books, doll houses, kitchenware, educational materials, clothes. Catalog - $2.50.

Christian Teaching Materials Company
14275 Elm Avenue
PO Box 639
Glenpool OK 74033-0639
(918)322-3420

- A selection of Christian and general teaching materials.

Covent Christian Services
85 Azalea Dr.
Eugene OR 97404

- Math minipulatives, science kits, etc.

Elijah Company
PO Box 12483
Knoxville TN 37912-0483
(615)475-7500

- General curriculum with informative descriptions.

The Family Educator
PO Box 309
Templeton CA 93465

- Phonics programs, texts, classic literature.

God's World Publications
PO Box 2330
Ashville NC 28802

- Classic literature biographies, and picture books. Graded monthly newspapers with Christian world view.

The Great Christian Books
229 South Bridge St.
Elkton MD 21922-8000

- Curriculum, textbooks, games, cassettes, and more.

Home Delivery Christian Library
223-A Montgomery Place
Conroe TX 77384
(409)273-2012

- A library by mail. Catalog and information packet $5.00.

The Home School Books and Supplies
3131 Smokey Pt. Drive
Arlington WA 98223
(206)659-6188

Life Time Gifts and Books
3900 Chalet Suzanne Dr.
Lake Wales FL 33853

- "The Always Incomplete Catalog" — hundreds of items.

Sycamore Tree
2179 Meyer Place
Costa Mesa CA 92627
(714)650-4466

- Books, science kits, arts and crafts kits, test preparation materials, school forms, assignment sheets, and much more.

Rainbow Re-source Center
610 E. Elm St.
PO Box 365
Taylorville IL 62568

- Buy and sell used curriculums and books.

Smarty Pants Educational Resources
1911 SW Park Forest
Lake Oswego OR 97034

- Multi-sensory materials and more.

Titus Woman's Potpourri
10817 NE 45th St.
Kirkland WA 98033
(206)388-4887

- New and used curriculum.

Toys to Treasure
4313-D Morgan Ave. East
Evansville IN 47715
(812)477-2703

- Homeschool family business. Games, etc.

Books About Christian Homeschooling

To obtain books, check with your Christian support group, local library, or Christian book store.

A Survivor's Guide to Home Schooling, by Luanne Shackelford and Susan White. A humorous look at homeschooling dilemmas.

Beautiful Girlhood, by Karen Andreola, 1993. Great Expectations, PO Box 2067, Eugene OR 97402. Encouraging young girls to high ideals.

The Big Book of Home Learning, by Mary Pride, 1987, four volume set in 1990. Getting Started; Preschool and Elementary; Teen and Adult; Afterschooling. The author reviews many secular and Christian educational materials from all sources. Mary tends to like quality materials that make learning fun for children, and she pulls no punches in describing what she likes and why.

The Christian Home Educator's Curriculum Manual, by Cathy Duffy. Help in choosing curriculum materials. Available from Home Run Enterprises, 12531 Aristocrat Ave, Garden Grove CA 92641. $16.95. Help in choosing materials to fit the child's learning style.

The Christian Home School, by Gregg Harris. Beginning book for Christian homeschoolers. *The Christian Family's Complete Household Organizer*, by Gregg and Sono Harris. A homeschool planner and record keeper. Both are available from Christian Life Workshops, PO Box 2250, Gresham OR 97030.

Excellence in Teaching with the Seven Laws, by Carl Shafer. Basic principles of educating children based on Gregory's classic Seven Laws of Teaching.

For the Children's Sake, by Susan Schaeffer Macaulay. Enriching life through education. Based on the philosophy of Charlotte Mason.

Hints on Child Training, by Henry C. Trumbull, 1993. Great Expectations, PO Box 2067, Eugene OR 97402. Practical biblical advice on child training that will last a lifetime.

Home Education: Is It Working?, published by H.O.P.E. for Texas. Pamphlet of graphs and statistics supporting the success of home education. Contact: PO Box 43887, Austin TX 78745.

Home School Burnout, by Raymond and Dorothy Moore. The Moore Foundation, PO Box 1, Camas WA 98607. Deals with problems faces by homeschoolers, including descriptions of homeschooling families. Also by the Moores: *Better Late Than Early, School Can Wait, Home Grown Kids, Home Spun Schools,* and *Home Style Teaching*.

The Home School Manual, by Ted Wade. This book includes an extensive appendix of resources and takes a structured approach to teaching and curriculum. 1993 revision. Gazelle Publications, 1906 Niles-Buchanan Rd., Niles MI 49120.

Home Schooling and the Law, by Michael Farris. Discusses the constitutional right to homeschool. Also *The Homeschooling Father*. Available from HSLDA, Box 159, Peaonian Springs VA 22129.

How to Tutor, by Samuel Blumenfeld. Information on one-to-one instruction for arithmetic, phonetic reading, and cursive writing.

Recovering the Lost Tools of Learning, by Douglas Wilson. Classical system of education as outlined by Dorothy Sayers. Crossway Books.

The Right Choice, by Christopher Klicka. Critique of public education with biblical and legal explanations of homeschooling. HSLDA, Box 159, Paeonian Springs VA 22129.

Teaching Children, by Diane Lopez. A scripturally based curriculum guide for K-6.

You Can Teach Your Child Successfully, by Dr. Ruth Beechick. Education Services, 8825 Blue Mountain Dr., Golden CO 80403. A guide for teaching your child grades 4-8. Other Beechick books include: *A Biblical Psychology of Learning, Parent-Help Series, a K-3 parent manual, A Home Start in Reading, A Strong Start in Language, An Easy Start in Arithmetic, Adam and His Kin*.

Why So Many Christians Are Going Home to School, by Llewellyn B. Davis. Provides justification for your decision to school at home. 1990, The Elijah Company, PO Box 12483, Knoxville TN 37912.

What the Bible Says About Child Training, by Richard Fugate. A biblical look at discipline and child training.

CHAPTER 28

Jewish Resources

Thanks to Janie Levine for gathering resources of interest to Jewish homeschooling families in Oregon.

National Information Networks

Jewish Family Resource Center (JFRC)
PO Box 300
Benton City WA 99320
(509)588-5013

Jewish Home Educators' Network (JHEN)
Pam Glaser Ernstoff
2 Webb Rd.
Sharon MA 02067
(617)784-9091

- Information, resources, and networking are available through both groups. JFRC stresses family learning experiences, natural learning, and unit studies, as well as utilizing community resources. JHEN has a similar slant, but leans more to the "child-centered" or unschooling philosophy.

The general listing that follows is appropriate for all Jewish families. For specific resources for the observant family, contact JFRC, above.

Resources

America's Jewish Bookstore
2028 Murray Ave.
Pittsburgh PA 15217-9946
(800)JUDAISM

A.R.E. Publishing, Inc.
3945 South Oneida St.
Denver CO 80237
(800)346-7779

Behrman House
235 Watchung Ave.
West Orange NJ 07052
(800)221-2755

Chadish Media LTD
453 East 9th St.
Brooksly NY 11218
(718)856-3882.

Davka Hebrew & Judaic Software
7074 N. Western Ave.
Chicago IL 60645
(800)621-8227

ERGO Home Video
668 Front Street
PO Box 2037
Teaneck NJ 07666
(201)692-0404

Kabbalah Software
8 Price Drive
Edison NJ 08817
(908)572-0869

The Learning Plant
PO Box 17233
West Palm Beach FL 33416
(407)686-2415

Nefesh Ami
PO Box 651
Hicksville NY 11801
(516)933-2660

Tara Publications
29 Derby Ave.
Cedarhurst NY 11516
(516)295-2290

Torah Aura Productions
4423 Fruitland Ave.
Los Angeles CA 90058
(800)BE-TORAH

Torah Umesorah Publications
5723 Eighteenth Ave.
Brooklyn NY 11204
(718)259-1223

CHAPTER 29

Muslim Resources

Thanks to Halimah Moustafa of IHSANA who offers these resources to the Islamic homeschooling community in Oregon.

Islamic Homeschool Association of North America
13320 SW Allen Ave. # 8
Beaverton OR 97005
(503)520-1901

- National contact for Islamic information and resources.

The Muslim Family
IHSANA
1312 Plymouth Court
Raleigh NC 27610

- A bi-monthly newsletter published by the Islamic Homeschool Association. To subscribe, send $10 to IHSANA. You will also receive a copy of *Muslim Guide to Home Education.*

❖

Catalogs

Arab World and Islamic Resources (AWAIR)
2095 Rose St. Ste. 4
Berkeley CA 94709
(510)704-0517

- Non-profit; educational materials for social studies teachers.

Sound Vision
843 W. Van Buren, Ste. 411
Chicago IL 60607
(800)432-4262

- "Helping tomorrow's Muslims today." Non-profit organization. Videos, books, tapes, software, and games.

IQRA' International Education Foundation (IIEF)
831 S. Laflin St.
Chicago IL 60607
(708)759-4981
Fax: (708)782-4520
(800)51-4272

- This organization is developing a comprehensive system of Islamic education, integrated curriculum, and an open university system. Over 40 books and 23 educational products, including complete preschool and kindergarten curriculums.

Halalco Books
108 E. Fairfax St.
Falls Church VA 22046
(703)532-3202
Fax: (703)241-0035

Islamic Book Service
(317)839-8150
(317)839-7669

American Muslim Resource Directory
PO Box 5670
Bel Ridge MO 63121

❖

Tapes And Videos

Adam's World (Series) from Sound Vision

- An Islamic version of "Sesame Street."

Children of the World and **Family Life,** by Wilmore Sadiki
Sadiki Enterprises
PO Box 611
Clearwater FL 34615
(813)447-6592

- Original songs written and performed by Wilmore Sadiki and family; acoustic; appropriate for all ages. They also offer a catalog, songbook, and other tapes.

Books - Young Children

The Day of Ahmad's Secret, by Florence Parry Heide and Judith Heide Gilliand. Lothrop, Lee and Shepard. 1990.

Muslim Nursery Rhymes, by Mustafa McDermott. Islamic Foundation, 1990. American Trust Publishing.

Karim and Fatimah, by Zeba Siddiqui.

- Read-aloud chapter book for the entire family. Great "Notes to Parents" section.

Ramadan Adventure of Fasfoose Mouse

Grandma's Garden

Books - Elementary

Great Friend of Children, The Brave Boy, The Broken Idol, The Desert Chief, Kingdom of Justice, The Long Search, The Longing Heart, Love All Creatures, Love at Home, Love Your Brother, Love Your Neighbor, Love Your God, The Persecutor Comes Home, Stories of the Caliphs, and *The Wise Poet.*

- This series is available from the Islamic Foundation in Britain. Storybooks are available with or without an audio cassette. This series is full of stories about the Prophet Muhammad, his closest companions, and other Muslims. The tapes were professionally recorded by Yusuf Islam (formerly Cat Stevens).

Islam for Children, by Ahmed von Denffer. The Islamic Foundation.

- Includes some activities and games.

Teachings of Our Prophet: A Selection of Ahadith for Children, by Dr. A. Ghazi and T. Ghazi, IQRA 1991.

- Translation and transliteration provided along with the original Arabic.

Our Prophet (Part 1 and 2).

- Part of the comprehensive curriculum developed by IQRA. Developmentally appropriate. Workbooks available.

Books - Intermediate

Mercy to Mankind (Part 1 and 2). IQRA, 1988. Workbooks available.

The Muslim Family Reader, Vol. 1 and 2, by Dr. Saidi El-Liwaru and Maisha Zoja El-Liwaru. 1988, American Trust Publishing.

- Designed to be read aloud for family discussion.

Tahdhib (Moral Education) and Sirah. Tawhid and Fiqh (Belief and Jurisprudence), by B. Aisha Lemu. Islamic Educational Trust, Nigeria.

- Concise, clear lessons in a logical sequence. Can be used in group instruction or by independent readers. Developmentally appropriate.

Companions of The Prophet, by Abdul Wahid Hamid, 1982, Umran Publishers. Three volumes.

- Sixty inspiring biographies of the first Muslim men and women; includes glossary, chronology, and maps.

Invincible Abdullah, by Haji Uthman Hutchinson.

- Hardy Boys style book - ages 10-14.

When we lose the right to be different,
we lose the privilege to be free.
—CHARLES EVANS HUGHES

Appendixes

APPENDIX A:

APPENDIX B:

APPENDIX C:

APPENDIX D:

Responsibility educates.
—Wendell Phillips

Appendix A
Legal Authority

Oregon Revised Statutes

ORS 339.010 School attendance required; age limits. Except as provided in ORS 339.030, all children between the ages of 7 and 18 years who have not completed the 12th grade are required to attend regularly a public full-time school of the school district in which the child resides.

ORS 339.020 Duty to send children to school. Except as provided in ORS 339.030, every person having control of any child between the ages of 7 and 18 years who has not completed the 12th grade is required to send such child to and maintain such child in regular attendance at a public full-time school during the entire school term.

ORS 339.030 Exemptions from compulsory school attendance. In the following cases, children shall not be required to attend public full-time schools: . . .

(3) Children being taught for a period equivalent to that required of children attending public schools by a parent or private teacher the course of study usually taught in grades 1-12 in the public school.

ORS 339.035 Teaching by private teacher or parent; notice; examination; effect of failure; appeal. (1) As used in this section, unless the context requires otherwise, "superintendent" means the executive officer of the education service district or the county school district serving the school district of which the child is a resident.

(2) Before a child is taught by a parent or private teacher, as provided in ORS 339.030, the parent or private teacher must notify the superintendent in writing. The superintendent shall acknowledge receipt of the notification in writing and inform the superintendent of the school district of the child's residence. The notification must be received and acknowledged before a child is withdrawn from school and thereafter before the start of each school year.

(3) Children being taught as provided in subsection (2) of this section shall be examined annually in the work covered in accordance with the following procedures:

(a)The State Board of Education shall adopt by rule a list of approved comprehensive examinations which are readily available.

(b) The parent shall select an examination from the approved list and arrange to have the examination administered to the child by a qualified neutral person, as defined by rule by the State Board of Education.

(c) The parent shall submit the results of the examination or the completed examination to the superintendent. If a completed examination is submitted, the superintendent shall have it scored and shall notify the parent of the results.

(d) If the superintendent determines after examining the results of the examination that the child is not showing satisfactory educational progress, as defined by rule by the State Board of Education, the superintendent may order the parent or other person having control of the child to send the child to school for the remainder of the school year.

(e) The parent or other person having control of the child may appeal the order to the Superintendent of Public Instruction, whose decision in the matter may be appealed to the circuit court.

ORS 339.460 Home school students authorized to participate in interscholastic activities; conditions.

(1) Home school students shall not be denied by a school district the opportunity to participate in all interscholastic activities if the student fulfills the following conditions:

(a) The student must be in compliance with all rules governing home schooling and shall provide the school administration with acceptable documentation of compliance.

(b) The student must meet all school district eligibility requirements with the exception of:

(A) The school district's school or class attendance requirements; and

(B) The class requirements of the voluntary association administering interscholastic activities.

(c) The student must achieve a minimum score on the achievement test required annually of all home schooling students which shall be taken at the end of each year, and which shall be used to determine eligibility for the following year. The minimum, composite test score, to be determined by the State Board of Education, shall not be higher than the 50th percentile as based on national norms.

(d) Any public school student who chooses to be home schooled must also meet the minimum test standards as described in paragraph (c) of this subsection. The student may participate while awaiting test results.

(e) Any public school student who has been unable to maintain academic eligibility shall be ineligible to participate in interscholastic activities as a home school student for the duration of the school year in which the student becomes academically ineligible and for the following year. The student must take required tests at the end of the second year and meet the standards described in paragraph (c) of this subsection to become eligible for the third year.

(f) The home school student shall be required to fulfill the same responsibilities and standards of behavior and performance, including related class or practice requirements, of other students participating in the interscholastic activity of the team or squad and shall be required to meet the same standards for acceptance on the team of squad. The home school student must also comply with all public school requirements during the time of participation.

(g) A home school student participating in interscholastic activities must reside with the attendance boundaries of the school for which the student participates.

(2) As used in this section:

(a) "Board" means the State Board of Education.

(b) "Home school students" are those children taught by private teachers or parents as described in ORS 339.035.

(c) "Interscholastic activities" includes but is not limited to athletics, music, speech, and other related activities. [1991 c.914 1, 2]

339.990 Penalties. Violation of ORS 339.020 or the requirements of ORS 339.035 is a Class B infraction. [Amended by 1965 c.100 299; 1967 c.67 10; 1985 c.597 3; 1993 c.413 1]

Oregon Administrative Rules

OAR 581-21-026
Examination of Children Instructed by Parent or Private Teacher

(1)　　　The following definitions and abbreviations apply to OAR 581-21-026 through 581-21-028 unless otherwise specified within the rule:

　　　(a)　　　"Child"; A person aged 7-18 whose parent or parents seek exemption from compulsory attendance under ORS 339.030(3).

　　　(b)　　　"Department" means the Oregon Department of Education.

　　　(c)　　　"Neutral person" means an individual selected by the parent or guardian of the child to be taught at home who has no relationship by bloodline or marriage to the child.

　　　(e)　　　"Notification" means written notice containing:

　　　　　　(A)　　　The child's and the parent's name, address, telephone number,

　　　　　　(B)　　　The child's birthdate, and

　　　　　　(C)　　　The name of the school the child is presently attending, or last attended, or if the child has not attended school, the name of the public school district in which the child resides.

　　　(e)　　　"Order" means to provide formal written notice in conformance with ORS 339.035 (3)(d).

　　　(f)　　　"Parent" is the natural parent or legal guardian of a child whom the parent desires to be exempted from compulsory attendance under the provisions of ORS 339.030(3).

　　　(g)　　　"Qualified person" is an individual who:

　　　　　　(A)　　　Holds a current personnel service certificate or teaching certificate from Oregon Teacher Standards and Practice Commission, or

　　　　　　(B)　　　Has been licensed by the Oregon Board of Psychologist Examiners, or

　　　　　　(C)　　　Has met the publisher's qualifications for purchase, and has purchased at least one test from the list set forth in Section (3) of this rule, or

　　　　　　(D)　　　Provides evidence of satisfactory completion of a graduate course in which test administration and interpretation is included in the objective, or

　　　　　　(E)　　　Has previously qualifies as a tester pursuant to Section (1)(g)(A) of this rule, and has during the previous year administered at least one test from the list set forth in Section (3) of this rule.

　　　(h)　　　"Satisfactory Educational Progress" means that, compared to the norming group for a test selected from the list in section (3) of this rule, the student scores at or above the 15th percentile (Normal Curve Equivalent (NCE) Score = 28) on the composite score of the selected test or, if the student scores below the 15th percentile, the student's composite score is equal to or greater than the composite score of the previous year.

(i)   "Superintendent" is the executive officer of the education service district (ESD) or where there is no ESD, the county school district serving the school district of which the child is a resident.

(2)   The parent or private teacher shall give written notification of intent to withdraw the child from school to the Superintendent at least 10 calendar days prior to the intended date of withdrawal each school year or at least 10 calendar days prior to the beginning of each school year. The Superintendent, within 10 calendar days of receipt of the notification, shall acknowledge receipt of same in writing to the parent and inform the superintendent of the child's resident district.

(3)   The parent must select the age-appropriate level of any one of the following tests to be administered to the child annually. A parent may choose to have a child initially tested beginning at age 7 with an oral or written first or second grade test. Test results used to satisfy the testing requirements of one year cannot be resubmitted in a succeeding year, nor may any equivalent test and norm be repeated to satisfy the testing requirements of the succeeding year except when a spring test score is used as the initial score. When the initial test is a spring test administered on or after March 1, that test score may be submitted for both the initial reporting requirement and the following fall (October 31) requirement contained in Section (6) of this rule.

      (a) California Achievement Test, 1977 or 1985, or 1992;

      (b) Comprehensive Tests of Basic Skills, 1981 or 1989;

      (c) Iowa Tests of Basic Skills/Tests of Achievement and Proficiency, 1982 or 1990;

      (d) Metropolitan Achievement Battery, 1985;

      (e) SRA Achievement Battery 1985;

      (f) Stanford Achievement Test Battery, 1982 or 1989; and

      (g) Tests adopted or approved by the State Board of Education that qualify for use in the required statewide assessment of students attending public schools.

(4)   The State Superintendent and the Oregon Department of Education shall make available a list of the publisher and address of each test.

(5)   The Department shall make available a list of persons qualified to administer tests under Subsection (1)(g) of this rule, such list to be updated by July 1 of each year. To be placed on the list, an applicant shall submit to the State Superintendent of Public Instruction evidence that satisfies requirements of Subsection (1)(g) of this rule.

(6)   If the test administrator scores the test, the administrator shall submit results of the test to the parents and provide a duplicate copy for the parent to submit to the Superintendent. If the test administrator does not score the test, the administrator shall submit the student answer sheet to the Superintendent whereupon after scoring the Superintendent shall return the results of the examination to the parent. The documents required shall be submitted to the Superintendent:

(a)   By October 31 of the school year in which the child is withdrawn or within eight weeks of notification to the Superintendent of withdrawal of the child, whichever date is later, if the child has not received home schooling in the preceding school year; or

(b)   By October 31 of the school year if the child has received home schooling in the preceding school year.

(7)   The test administrator shall certify that the administrator is qualified and neutral as defined in this rule with respect to a child being tested.

(8)   All costs for the test instrument, administration, and scoring are the responsibility of the parent. If the completed but unscored document is submitted to the Superintendent, the Superintendent shall have the test scored for which a fee may be charged.

(9)   The parent shall submit the results of the examination, the name of the test administrator and the test administrator's statement certifying qualification and neutrality to the Superintendent by October 31 of the school year in which the child is withdrawn or within eight weeks of notification to the Superintendent of withdrawal of the child, whichever date is later.

(10)   A child who turns seven after September 1 shall not be required to be tested, nor shall the parent be required to notify the Superintendent, until the beginning of the next school year.

(11)   Failure to submit the test results or completed test in accordance with Section (9) of this rule, shall be a basis for the Superintendent to notify the child's resident district that the parent has not met the requirements of ORS 339.035.

Statutory Authority: 339.030(3) and 339.035

dc OAR353
3/29/93

OAR 581-21-027
Determination of Satisfactory Educational Progress

(1)   Upon receipt of a child's test results, the superintendent shall provide a copy of the results to parents and shall make a determination whether satisfactory educational progress is being made by the child as defined in OAR 581-21-026(1)(i). No parent shall be ordered to send the child to school for the remainder of the school year based upon results of the first annual examination submitted by the parents for their child to meet requirements under ORS 339.035(3).

(2)   In the event that the superintendent finds that the child is not showing satisfactory educational progress, the superintendent shall provide the parent with a written statement of the reasons for the finding, based on the test results and may:

(a)   Order the parent to send the child to school for the remainder of the school year; or

(b)   Allow, with the consent of the parent, the child's education to be supervised by a person who holds a current Oregon teaching certificate for the remainder of the school year. The parent shall be responsible for the cost of services of the certificated person. The child's test results shall be submitted to the Superintendent by October 31 of the succeeding school year. If, upon receipt of the test results, the Superintendent finds that the child has failed to achieve satisfactory educational progress as defined in OAR 581-21-026(1)(i), the Superintendent may send the child to school for the remainder of that school year.

OAR 581-21-029
Home Schooling for Handicapped Students

(1)   The following definitions apply to OAR 581-21-029:

(a)   "District" means the school district of the parent's residence on the date of the notification of the superintendent by the parent or guardian of the intent to teach the child at home.

(b)   "Resident district superintendent" means the superintendent of the district as defined in subsection (1)(a) of this rule.

(c)   "Superintendent" means the executive officer of the Education Service District or, where there is not ESD, the county school district serving the school district of which the child is a resident.

(d)   "Parent" means the natural parent of legal guardian of a child whom the parent desires to be exempted from compulsory attendance under the provisions of ORS 339.030(5).

(c)   "Handicapped child" means a child meeting the eligibility criteria for their specific handicapping condition as set forth in OAR 581-15-051.

(2)   When a parent notifies the superintendent, as provided in OAR 581-21-025, that he/she intends to teach the child at home, the superintendent, in accordance with OAR 581-21-026, shall notify the resident district superintendent.

(3)   If the child is identified as handicapped, the district shall offer, and document to the parent, opportunities for the child to receive or continue to receive special education and related services. Such services, however, shall not be provided in the home.

(4)   If the child has been identified as handicapped and the parent refused special education services, the district shall:

(a)   Record the parent's refusal;

(b)   Document to the parent the availability of special education services for their child; and

(c)   For the students in a special education, send a notice of change of placement to the parent stating that the parent has elected to withdraw the child from public school under ORS 339.030(5). The notice shall include statements that:

(A)   The district has the responsibility to offer a free appropriate public education;

(B)   The district has offered the free appropriate public education;

(C)   The parent may request a due process hearing as provided under OAR 581-15-081; and

(D)   The child is entitled at any time to re-enroll in the public school.

(5)   If the parent, resident district superintendent or superintendent believes a child is handicapped the district shall follow procedures under OAR 581-15-039 to obtain parent consent for evaluation to determine the child's eligibility to receive special education and related services. If the child is eligible, the district shall notify the parent and shall offer the child a free appropriate public education.

(6)   If a parent of a child refuses consent for evaluation of the child, the district shall document the refusal and initiate due process hearing procedures under ORS 343.165 and OAR 581-15-080 through OAR 581-15-096:

(a)   If the parent participates in the hearing but refuses to comply with the decision of the hearings officer, the district shall document, in the hearing record, its attempt to evaluate, identify and offer the child a free appropriate education.

(b)   If the parent does not participate in the hearing, the district shall document, in the hearing record, its attempt to evaluate, identify and offer the child a free appropriate education and the parent's lack of consent thereto.

(c)   A child who has not been evaluated and identified, shall be considered nonhandicapped by the district.

(7)   Notwithstanding OAR 581-21-027 in determining satisfactory education progress for a handicapped child, the district shall direct the multi-disciplinary team to evaluate the child as required under OAR 581-15-072 to determine whether satisfactory educational progress appropriate to the age and handicapping condition of the child has been made:

(a)   In place of the child's regular teacher as specified in OAR 581-14-072(7)(a)(A), the multidisciplinary team shall include the parent, and the person teaching the child when such is the case.

(b)   The multidisciplinary team report shall state whether the child has made satisfactory educational progress, and the superintendent shall consider that report in determining the child's progress. The student need not complete all IEP goals in order for the superintendent to make a determination that the child is making satisfactory educational progress.

(c)   If the parent refuses the annual evaluation or refuses to arrange to have a test administered as required in ORS 339.035 and OAR 581-21-026 for nonhandicapped students, the superintendent shall follow procedures set out in OAR 581-21-026(10). The local district may take action against the parent for violation of ORS 339.035 or ORS 339.020.

(8)   The superintendent may order the child back to school if the child has not made satisfactory educational progress. The parent may appeal the order of the superintendent following procedures under OAR 581-21-028.

(April, 1987)

OAR 581-21-033
Interscholastic Activities Eligibility

Requirement for Home School Students

(1)   A home school student may participate in interscholastic activities in his or her resident district's attendance area if the student meets all of the requirements of ORS 339.460 and:

(a)   Achieves a composite test score that is not less than the 23rd percentile on any of the annual achievement tests listed in OAR 581-21-026; and

(b)   Submits the students composite test score to the district prior to participation in an interscholastic activity.

(2)   Notwithstanding subsection (1)(b) of this rule, any public school student who chooses to be home schooled may participate in interscholastic activities while awaiting test score results.

The best test of freedom
is perhaps less in what we are free to do than
in what we are free not to do.
--Eric Hoffer

Appendix B
Education Service Districts

The ESD is not your neighborhood school district of residence. The county-wide ESD offers a variety of services to all the school districts in your county, in addition to keeping homeschooling records. Several smaller counties without an ESD have a County Unit, which offers the services instead. Notification of intent to homeschool and student achievement test results are sent to the ESD or County Unit of the county in which you reside. This section includes testing services and any other materials and services that are offered by each ESD.

Baker County ESD
2100 Main St.
Baker 97814
523-5801
Contact: Ruth Whitnah, Superintendent

- Sends copies of law and administrative rules to parents that send notification. Stanford Achievement test is offered at $10 for the April group test, and $30 any other time. Local schools do not allow homeschooled students to take the test with them. Part-time participation in local schools is generally discouraged. Compiles a collection of textbook and instructional materials catalogs for homeschooling families to use. "I work well with homeschooling families and enjoy hearing of their successes!"

Clackamas County ESD
PO Box 216
Marylhurst 97036
635-0500
Contacts:
Arlene Gintz, Homeschooling Records Clerk, 635-0577
Steve Thompson, Director, Curr., Instr., & Eval., 635-0562

- Provides notification form, questions and answers, copies of law and administrative rules. Currently being revised. Some local districts make activities and resources available to homeschoolers, or allow part-time attendance. Provides test scoring for a fee. Willing to answer questions and help locate resources.

Clatsop County ESD
3194 Marine Dr.
Astoria 97103
325-2862
Richard Laughlin, Superintendent

• Provides letter of notification. No testing services. Offers textbooks, curriculum guides, staff help when requested. Homeschoolers may participate in school part-time, according to local district policy. "We think our relationship is well founded by past service."

Columbia County ESD
PO Box 900
800 Port Avenue
St. Helens 97051
397-0028
Contact: Verle Bechtel, Superintendent
or Kay Covel

• Provides brochure/notification form. No testing services.

Coos County ESD
1350 Teakwood Ave.
Coos Bay 97420
269-1611
Contact: Sharon Smith

• Provides informational brochure and notification form. No testing services.

Crook County Unit
1390 SE 2nd St.
Prineville 97754
447-3743
Contact: Linda Moling

• No written material provided. Homeschoolers may join the district-wide testing, using the Iowa Test of Basic Skills. Homeschoolers may participate in school on a part-time basis.

Curry County ESD
PO Box 786
Gold Beach 97444
247-6681, contact: Sam Wilson

• Provides an informational brochure. No testing services. Most local districts will allow part-time participation by homeschooled students. "We cooperate and have had a very successful experience with homeschoolers."

Deschutes County ESD
1340 NW Wall St.
Bend 97701
382-3171
Contact: Sharon Weber

• Booklet and notification forms provided. No testing service at this time.

Douglas County ESD
1871 NE Stephens St.
Roseburg 97470
440-4777
Contact: Sharon Horne

• Provides an informational brochure/notification form. No testing services.

Gilliam County ESD
PO Box 637
Condon 97823
384-2732
Contact: H. James Burton, Superintendent

• Homeschoolers are encouraged to take the yearly achievement tests (SRA) offered at the public school of residence. Local districts are encouraged to involve homeschoolers.

Grant County ESD
835-A South Canyon Blvd.
John Day 97845
575-1349

• Brochure provided. Offers CTB/4 testing on a strictly optional basis and notifies each registered homeschooling family. "This ESD provides as much assistance as we can given the fiscal and staff time limitations. All children are important and we assist as we can."

Harney County ESD
450 N Buena Vista Ave.
Burns 97720
573-2426
Ed Schumacher, Superintendent

• Notification form and procedure guidelines are available. They supply CTBS test materials. A Browsing Library of surplus textbooks and related resources is made available as a courtesy to homeschoolers. Call 573-2122 for office hours.

Hood River County SD
11th & Eugene Sts.
PO Box 920
Hood River 97031
386-2511
Contact: Suze Nigl, 387-5013

• Provides a handbook of information, including copies of the law, rules,
  tests, and testers. Homeschoolers are allowed to participate in the district-
  wide testing in the spring. With respect to part-time participation, Hood
  River has a "dual enrollment policy, but it was designed for private school
  students to participate in athletics - they have to take five classes." Staff
  are willing to help homeschoolers and resource materials are made accessi-
  ble. There is excellent communication with a majority of the home schooling parents.

Jackson County ESD
101 N. Grape St.
Medford 97501
776-8456
Shelby Price, Superintendent

• Provides an information packet. Does not offer testing, but homeschoolers
  may take the test given by individual districts. In Jackson County, children
  who participate in school on a part-time basis are considered to be enrolled
  rather than homeschooled. Some local districts offer additional services.
  The ESD has a vast instructional library but, by law, cannot lend directly to
  homeschoolers. A local district could request materials from the library,
  then loan them to homeschoolers. The ESD has an "honest, simple,
  straight, and positive" relationship with homeschooled persons.

Jefferson County ESD
1355 Buff St.
Madras 97741
475-6192, Cindy Harris

• Provides a parents guide to home instruction. Children receiving instruction in a privat or parochial school registered with the Oregon Department
  of Education is not considered to home instructed student. No testing services are provided, except for handicapped children.

Josephine County Unit
8550 New Hope Rd.
PO Box 160
Murphy 97533
862-3111
Contact: Sandy Varady

- If written materials are available at the area school, those are sometimes shared with parents. Testing services are available at the area school in April for $6.00. MAT test is used. Students living in remote, inaccessible areas are allowed to participate in school on a part-time basis.

Klamath County SD
2450 Summers Ln.
Klamath Falls 97603
883-5000

Lake County ESD
357 North L Street
Lakeview 97630
947-3371
Don Knowles, Superintendent

- Notification form and test information. Provides certified teachers with CTBS tests, then score the tests and inform parents of the results. The only expense would be whatever you pay the teacher for his time. Director of Special Programs will also administer tests. All programs provided through Lake ESD are available to homeschoolers. Textbooks and other services are provided as needed and if available.

Lane County ESD
PO Box 2680
1200 Highway 99 N.
Eugene 97402
689-6500

- Information packet includes a reference handout covering basic legal guidelines, an enrollment form, and a list of tests and qualified test administrators in Lane County.

Lincoln County SD
459 SW Coast Hwy.
PO Box 1110
Newport 97365
265-4403
Contact: Karen Clark, 265-4408

- Provides a list of homeschooling courses. Provides testing when the test they give satisfies home school requirements. Students are free to enroll on a part-time status for regular programs. Homeschoolers have access to audiovisual materials in the district Instructional Media Center. "We work with home school families on an individual basis. Spirit of cooperation and assistance."

Linn-Benton County ESD
905 4th Ave. SE
Albany 97321
967-8822
Contact: Bobbie Marple, Home School Secretary
or Dave Moore, Home School Coordinator

- Information packet includes law and administrative rules, lists of tests and testers, notification form. CTBS tests and scoring are provided to any qualified tester who requests them for a total of $10. On-site textbook library.

MalheurCounty ESD
PO Box 610
Vale 97918
473-3138
Contact: Judy Bishop

- Offers a packet of homeschooling information, including law, questions and answers regarding testing, notification form. Testing within the public school is provided for $4.00, plus $4.00 for scoring. Any qualified tester who requests a test will be provided MAT/6 tests for the same fee.

Marion County ESD
3400 Portland Rd. NE
Salem 97303
588-5330

- Provides informational brochure and a notification form in quadruplicate. No testing services. Most schools will allow part-time participation. "We encourage the parent/legal guardian to work closely with the school and to maintain a relationship with the public school system in developing a curriculum for the home school student."

Morrow County SD 1
270 W Main
PO Box 368
Lexington 97839
989-8202

Multnomah County ESD
11611 NE Ainsworth Circle
Portland 97220
255-1841
Contact: Gail Anderson, 257-1651

- Provides a brochure/notification form in question and answer form. No testing services provided. Local districts may administer tests or provide materials, but are not required to do so.

Polk County ESD
322 Main St.
Dallas 97338
623-6691

- Question and answer type brochure provided. No testing service available, although testing is provided by some local school districts.

Sherman County ESD
HCR 01 Box 95
Moro 97039
565-3509
Dale Coles, Superintendent

- Makes materials available as requested. Provides CTBS testing for homeschoolers in their resident school district at no charge. Individual schools generally allow some participation by homeschoolers. "We attempt to be open and willing to assist."

Tillamook County ESD
PO Box 416
Tillamook 97141
842-8423

Umatilla County ESD
PO Box 38
Pendleton 97801
276-6616

Union County ESD
10100 N. McAlister Rd.
La Grande 97850
963-4106
Contact: Wendy Simer, 963-4106

- Provides an information brochure and notification form for homeschoolers. Does not provide testing services; some local districts provide testing with their regular students and may charge for service to homeschoolers.

Wallowa County ESD
301 W. North St.
Enterprise 97828
426-4997

- No information or services are provided. Homeschoolers are referred to their local school district and can participate in classes on a part-time basis.

Wasco County ESD
422 E. Third St.
The Dalles 97058
298-5155
Contact: Ernie Keller or Mary Kramer, 298-5157

• Provides letter of intent, copy of law and ad. rules, question and answer information. No testing services available, but local district may provide testing, if requested, and may charge a fee.

WashingtonCounty ESD
17705 NW Springville Rd.
Portland 97229
690-5400
Contact: Melanie McBain

• Offers a packet of copies of homeschooling law and administrative rules, tests, testers, and a notification form. Homeschoolers may be able to arrange to participate part-time in the local school. Does not offer testing.

Wheeler County ESD
PO Box 206
Fossil 97830
763-4384

Yamhill County ESD
800 E. Second St.
McMinnville 97128
472-1431
Contact: Mary Kerns or Janine

• Offers a brochure. Offers CTBS testing to all - $40 per student with a discount for family.

Appendix C

Approved Tests And Test Publishers

The tests that have been approved for use by homeschooled students in Oregon are listed below. The tests vary in availability, length, and difficulty.

• California Achievement Test, 1977, 1985, or 1992
    The CAT (SURVEY), for grades 1 - 12, takes only two to three hours. The complete battery takes four to six hours.

• Comprehensive Tests of Basic Skills, 1981 or 1989
    CTB/McGraw-Hill Order Services Center, 2500 Garden Road, Monterey CA 93940, (800)538-9547

• Iowa Tests of Basic Skills/Tests of Achievement and Proficiency, 1982 or 1990
    The Riverside Publishing Company Customer Service, 8420 Bryn Mawr Avenue, Chicago IL 60631(800)323-9540

• Metropolitan Achievement Battery, 1985

Stanford Achievement Test Battery, 1985, Psychological Corporation, 1250 6th Avenue, San Diego CA 60631, (619)669-6592

• SRA Achievement Battery, 1978 or 1985
    Order: SRA, PO Box 5380, Chicago IL 60680, (800)621-0476
    Quotation Request: SRA 155 N. Wacker Drive, Chicago IL 60606

• Also approved for use by homeschooled students in Oregon are tests adopted or approved by the State Board of Education that qualify for use in the required statewide assessment of students attending public schools.

Individuality is either the mark of genius or the reverse.
Mediocrity finds safety in standardization.
—Frederick E. Crane

Appendix D
Test Administrators

     Qualified test administrators are individuals who hold a current personnel service or teaching certificate; or who have been licensed by the Oregon Board of Psychologist Examiners; or who have purchased, from the publisher, at least one test from the Test List; or who provide evidence of satisfactory completion of a graduate course in which test administration and interpretation is included in the objective. Each tester receives a letter stating that he is qualified, and is then placed on the state approved list of testers. The list is updated annually on July 1. An asterisk (*) indicates testers who are not available for general testing. A double asterisk (**) indicates testers who are known to be qualified, but who qualified after the 1993 list was published by the Department of Education.

     All school districts and ESD personnel meeting the requirement of a "Qualified Person" are authorized to test through their agency. School districts and ESDs are not obligated to conduct testing of homeschoolers.

     You can choose any tester from the list, not just the ones who reside in your county. A few qualified testers live in the bordering state of Washington as well. Homeschooled students must be tested by a "neutral person," that is, someone who has no relationship to the student by bloodline or marriage.

BAKER

Baker ESD
2100 Main
Baker 97814
523-5801

BENTON

Marshall Adams
1110 NW 30th
Corvallis 97330
752-1067

Holly Olsen
27114 Hayden Rd
Alsea 97324
487-7340

Roger Brownell
1140 NW Lester Ave.
Corvallis 97330

Andy Covitz
7429 1/2 NW Mt. View
Drive
Corvallis 97330

Carolyn Gardner
3223 NW McKinley
Corvallis 97330

N. Victoria Gnose
636 NW 21st St.
Corvallis 97330
753-8975

Erik Knoder
3830 Country Club
Corvallis 97333
757-8480

Marcia Ridpath
226 NE Azalea Dr.
Corvallis 97330

Melinda R. Sayavedra
1463 NW Tyler Ave.
Corvallis 97330

Christine Smith
721 SW 16th
Corvallis 97330

Karen Sundseth
1765 NW Arthur Circle
Corvallis 97330

Alberta J. Thyfault
935 NW Hobard Ave.
#43
Corvallis 97330
737-6388

CLACKAMAS

Kenda Alexander
13760 SE Orient Dr.
Boring 97009
668-7685

Deborah Breese-Tyler
4597 Black Forest Ct.
Lake Oswego 97035

Basic Skills Assessment
Service
Curt Bumcrot
Jenny Bumcrot
16652 S. Annette Drive
Oregon City 97038
650-5282

Bonita Crumley
50170 SE Cherryville
Dr.
Sandy 97055

Marilyn Donovan
4355 Riverview St., #3
West Linn 97061

* Nancy Duhrkoop
16811 S. Pam Drive
Oregon City 97045
656-3470

Donna J. Lane
15710 S. Redland Rd.
Oregon City 97405

* Luanna Meuser
10140 S. Hwy 211
Canby 97013
651-3116

Amanda Middlebrooks
923 Woodlawn
Oregon City 97045
650-0862

Eleanor Ray
29383 SW Grahams
Ferry Rd.
Wilsonville 97070

Barbara Schnoor
13080 SE Geneva Way
Portland 97236

Julie Ziegler
15821 SE Naef Ct.
Milwaukie 97267
659-5295

CLATSOP

Pamela Bierly
120 12th Ave.
Seaside 97138

Michael Leamy
Rt. 1 Box 901
Astoria 97103
325-6432

Anita McKenzie
917 Grand
Astoria 97103
325-1724

COLUMBIA

Constance Bennett
56692 Mollenhour Rd.
Scappoose 97056
543-2437

Harriet Curtis
28778 Parkdale Rd.
Rainier 97048
556-9715

Mary Scherzinger
200 Sunset Blvd. Apt. 1
St. Helens 97051
397-5913

COOS

* Karen Dorsey
1564 East Bay Dr.
North Bend 97459
756-4494

C. Delores Finkbeiner
1850 Clark Street
North Bend 97459
756-1411

Gladys Shires
1850 Clark Street
North Bend 97459
756-1411

Jo Anne Walker
1850 Clark Street
North Bend 97459
756-1411

Diana Younker
1850 Clark Street
North Bend 97459
756-1411

CROOK

Peggy Miller (Karrle)
765 S Garner
Prineville 97754
447-6825

CURRY

Glenda Wilber
PO Box 2231
Harbor 97415
469-5231

DESCHUTES

Mildred Babcock
HC 76 Box 1047
LaPine 97426

Mary Y. Bickers
1512 N. Canyon Drive
Redmond 97756

Mark Holiday
55165 River Forest Ln.
Bend 97707-2414

Gregg Marron
1340 NW Wall St.
Bend 97701
382-3171

Morris Martin
22310 Rickard Rd.
Bend 97702

Joy Mosier
19871 Robinwood Pl.
Bend 97702
389-6743

Arnold Powelson
60631 Devon Circle
Bend 97702
389-1901

Diana Prichard
PO Box 555
Sisters 97759

Tracy Viall-Link
1353 NE Noe Dr.
Bend 97701

DOUGLAS

Karen Combs
940 Becker Rd.
Roseburg 97470
673-7233

Molly Jacobsen
120 Winston Section
Rd.
Winston 97496

Judy Ode
700 Terri Ct.
Winston 97496
679-9677

* Carol Sumerlin
PO Box 325
Days Creek 97429
825-3014

Leon Stansfield
2079 NW Witherspoon
Ave.
Roseburg 97470
672-2199

Sue Windsor
115 Kermanshah
Roseburg 97470
679-4138

GILLIAM

None

GRANT

None

HARNEY

Harney ESD
PO Box 72
Burns 97220
573-2426

Joseph Hendry
Star Rt. 2, 102 Oilwell Rd.
Burns 97720

HOOD RIVER

Scott Winters
823 Eugene St.
Hood River 97031
386-4421

JACKSON

Phyllis Berger
42 S.. Barneburg Rd.
Medford 97504

Brenda Lee Cotta
2433 Huntington Lane
Medford 97504
776-0435

Pamela Dickson
910 Vista Park Dr.
Eagle Point 97524

* Dixie Ann Fitch
718 Sardine Creek Rd.
Gold Hill 97525

David Flood
1719 Rine St.
Medford 97501

* Linda Hall
100 Wilson Rd.
Central Point 97502
644-4935

* Mae Anne Heide
1057 Janes Road
Medford 97501

P. Isabel Hillock
44 Church Street
Ashland 97520
482-7268

* Denise E. Keenan
PO Box 351
Jacksonville 97530

* Jean Maxwell
458 West Pine St.
Central Point 97502
664-3231

Marilyn McArty
600 Green Tree Lp
Grants Pass 97527

Dennis Ortman
2441 Obispo Dr.
Medford 97504

Nellieann Ragsdale
PO Box 95
Butte Falls 97522

Deborah Reed
649 Crater Lake Ave.
Medford 97504
772-1438

Ron Reed
7629 Gold Ray Rd
Central Point 97504

Janet Snyder
13440 Highway 234
Gold Hill 97525

JEFFERSON

Carolyn Herringshaw
8710 SW Elbe Dr.
Culver 97734
546-6171

JOSEPHINE

* Josephine Co. SD
PO Box 160
Murphy 97533
862-3111

Frode Jensen
1355 Ferry Rd.
Grants Pass 97526
476-3080

Marilyn McCarty
600 Green Tree Loop
Grants Pass 97527
479-5988

Celestia Riordan
207 NE Terry Ln.
Grants Pass 97526

Midge Shaw
275 Potts Way
Grants Pass 97526
479-9649

* Laurie Taft
848 Bull Creek Rd.
Grants Pass 97527
479-0645

KLAMATH

Joel Brain
31676 Modoc Point Rd.
Chiloquin 97624

Sharon Chappell
HC 30 Box 1458
Chiloquin 97624
783-2908

Mike Fimbres
931 Kane St.
Klamath Falls 97603
884-7521

Carol LeQuieu
3814 Madison St.
Klamath Falls 97601
884-2830

LANE

Laurie Cardwell
1154 S 44th
Springfield 97478
746-2462

Louise Chilson
18400 Pataha Creek Rd.
Walton 97490
935-3420

Rose Ann Coe
659 S. 44th St.
Springfield 97478
726-6063

Clayton Crymes
1755 Graham Dr.
Eugene 97405

M. Suzanne Crymes
1775 Graham Dr.
Eugene 97405

Robert Crymes
1775 Graham Dr.
Eugene 97405

Deana Graham
31126 Lanes Turn Rd.
Eugene 97401

Zehra Faye Greenleaf
674 W. 24th Place
Eugene 97405

Ellen Hampton
3219 Tilden Street
Eugene 97404
688-2249

Vicky Heyen
80297 Hwy. 99N.
Cottage Grove 97424

Debra D. Jaffarian
2074 Todd St.
Eugene 97405

Brenda Johnson
2505 W. 22nd Ave.
Eugene 97405
344-1054

Sherry Lyons
PO Box 1224
Florence 97439
997-2161

Brenda Magee
90350 Hill Rd.
Springfield 97478

Ardyth McGrath
466 Azalea Ave. W.
Eugene 97404

Diane Sontag
151 N Grand #1
Eugene 97440
687-4664

Kathy Smith
32112 Latham School
Cottage Grove 97424

Laurie Walz
1018 Martha Ct.
Eugene 97401
485-0725

* Marilee Workentin
982 Waite St.
Eugene 97402
689-9482

LINCOLN

Kathryn Taylor
842 SW Goverment St.
Newport 97365
265-5817

LINN

Janelle C. Barnett
43933 McDowell Creek
Dr.
Lebanon 97355

Sandra K. Bird
P.O. Box 55
Brownsville 97327

Keith W. Cantrell
928 13th Ave.
Sweet Home 97386

Rebecca Copeland
36009 Tennessee Road
Albany 97321

Sarah P. Haley
900 W. 10th #8
Lebanon 97355

Arzalea Mae Hostetler
29021 Highway 99E
Shedd 97377

Lana Kelly
1365 Morse Lane SW
Albany 97321
928-0796

Deborah Martin
PO Box 183
Lebanon 97355
451-3360

Ann Puig
1080 Eddie St.
Lebanon 97355
258-3854

Jeffry Stolsig
38033 Weirich Drive
Lebanon 97355

Marjorie Dee Wallace
611 West "D" St.
Lebanon 97355

Valerie Weaver
39150 Griggs Drive
Lebanon 97355
451-2443

Susan Wilkinson
420 SE Third Ave.
Albany 97321
928-1110

MALHEUR

Nancy Allen
348 Grove Road
Ontario 97914

MARION

John Cavender
20575 Ferry Rd. SE
Stayton 97383
859-3531

Patricia L. Chalupsky
43415 Kingston Lyons
Dr.
Stayton 97383

Mary Halter
20921 Olmstead Rd.
NE
Aurora 97002
678-1811

Jane Horner
7050 Wheatland Rd. N.
Keizer 97303

Mary McRae
1803 Kent Ave.
Stayton 97383
769-4882

Ed Meier
813 Teton Ct. SE
Salem 97301
364-0825

Georgia Meier
813 Teton Ct. SE
Salem 97301
364-0825

Margaret Palazzo
2035 Jelden St. NE
Salem 97303
362-6219

Irma Porter
1930 Hampden Lane
NE #22
Salem 97305
362-7121

Julie Ruscher
4540 Angie Marie Way
NE
Salem 97305

Hazel Spees
12465 Meridian Rd. NE
Mt. Angel 97362
634-2421

Kathleen Summers
10933 Summit Lp. Rd.
Turner 97392

Mark Timmons
4060 Filbert St. NE
Salem 97303

Ginger Welter
189 E. Washington St.
Stayton 97383

MORROW

None

MULTNOMAH

Winnifred Allum
1201 SE 209th Ave.
Gresham 97030
666-6473

Judy K. Coleman
4635 NE 112th
Portland 97220

Wilma Crabtree
16901 SE Division, #5
Portland
761-5410

David Crymes
1426 SE 120th
Portland 97216

Charlene Holzwarth
2524 NE 34
Portland 97212
284-3444

Julane Jenison
11805 SE Madison
Portland 97216

** Ann Lahrson
PO Box 80214
Portland 97280
244-9677

Christopher Meisinger
4009 SE 48th St.
Portland 97206

* Fred Morton
5827 NE 14th Ave.
Portland 97211

Jane Popkin
7546 SW Aloma Wy #5
Portland 97223

* H. B. Sligar
9201 NE Fremont
Portland 97213
252-5207

Susan L. Thomas
9590 SW Wilshire St.
Portland 97225

* Alison Turner
1834 NE 90th Ave.
Portland 97220
254-2248

**Christine Webb
11622 SW 33rd. Pl.
Portland 97219
245-7430

* Marcia Workentine
2853 NE 56th Ave.
Portland 97213
281-8041

Judith Yerion
10330 NE Beech St.
Portland 97220
256-4240

POLK

Jenny Barth
245 NW Hillcrest
Dallas 97338
623-4782

Ruth Berger
15050 Oakdale Road
Dallas 97338
623-3070

Jeanne Cannon
287 Warren St. North
Monmouth 97361
838-3489

Linda Dalke
12615 Fishback Rd.
Monmouth 97361

TILLAMOOK

Anita Townsend
PO Box 646
Rockaway Beach 97136
355-2155

UMATILLA

Carolyn Cogswell
4450 SW Quinney
Pendleton 97801
276-8569

Catherine Duffy
935 E Gladys
Hermiston 97

Margaret Gass
Rt 2. Box 2331
Hermiston 97838

Linda Marquardt
7816 1/2 Flight Ave.
Los Angeles CA 90045
(213)645-9813

UNION

Barbara Ely
59674 Foothill Rd.
LaGrande 97850

Judith Collier
PO Box 132
LaGrande 97850
963-7352

Phyllis Hart
1102 12th St.
LaGrande 97850
963-8750

Marian Montgomery
505 Main
LaGrande 97850
963-7577

Heather Stanhope
70523 Follett Rd.
Elgin 97827
437-2330

WALLOWA

None

WASCO

Candace Cannon
Rt. 1 Box 441
Maupin 97037
395-2589

Bernie Chastain
Rt. 1 Box 135
Maupin 97037

* Candace Smith
79779 Shellrock Rd.
Dufur 97021
467-2258

WASHINGTON

Washington ESD
17705 NW Springville
Rd.
Portland 97229

Barbara Anderson
18007 SW Belton Rd.
Sherwood 97140

Bonnie Heinz
11540 SW Manzanita
St.
Tigard 97223
684-2048

Margaret Lamb
11960 SW Settler Way
Beaverton 97005
524-6527

Richard McIntyre
18076 SW Arborcrest
Aloha 97006
649-2204

Mary Ann Merkel
3815 SW Hall Blvd.
Beaverton 97005
643-1195

Kathy Parish
Route 1 Box 281
Gaston 97119

Ilana Rembelinsky
2727 22nd Ave. #39
Forest Grove 97116
357-7130

** Sharon Rocha
22650 NW Moran Rd.
Hillsboro 97214
621-3791

Barbara Summey
2961 SE Cedar Dr.
Hillsboro 97123
648-0245

WHEELER

Julie Donnelly
Star Route
Spray 97874
462-3565

Keith Strom
Wheeler ESD, PO Box
206
Fossil 97830
763-4384

YAMHILL

Bonita Boyce
643 E. Main
Sheridan 97378
876-4388

Lanita Harkema
4215 NE Sokol Blosser
Dayton 97114
864-2082

Lela Mae Higgins
1103 N. Springbrook,
#17
Newberg 97132
538-1827

Connie Valesano
PO Box 265
817 S. Pine
Carlton 97111
852-6325

Harold Wilhite
1100 N. Meridian #19
Newberg 97132
538-3204

WASHINGTON STATE

Ida Edwards
PO Box 9
Washougal WA 98671
(206)835-8708

* Donald Whittle
PO Box 9
Washougal WA 98671
(206)835-9292

Acknowledgements

Simply stated, my gratitude to Kim Gordon is boundless. Without Kim's ideas, insights, and hard, hard work, this book would not have been written—period. Kim taught me an important lesson, and that is, if a resource does not exist, it should be created, so let's write a book. (And here it is — three years later!) Kim's words and ideas can be found throughout the book, although she will accept no credit. Her contributions to the vision and the sheer work, while notable throughout, are especially significant and appreciated in Chapters 1, 2, 8, 9, 18, and 27. Kim is a dear friend whose partnership in a project turns work into play.

I also want to thank some of the many others who have contributed to this book, directly or indirectly, including:

Christine Webb and Sharon Rocha, who proofread, edited, encouraged, and provided some terrific resources;

Sue Welch, Ranell Curl, Janie Levine, and Halimah Moustafa, for their assistance with Part Four;

Jane and Michael Fleming, and Ranell Curl, who have taught me valued lessons in give and take, and who have supported the writing of this book far beyond the demands of friendship;

Rick Lahrson, who believes in me, even now; whose insights and understanding are deeply appreciated; and whose technical support and computer knowledge are peerless;

And finally, thank you to all of my homeschooling friends, tall and small, who have inspired me, believed in me, and encouraged me from beginning to end.

Freedom rings where opinions clash.
—Adlai E. Stevenson

About The Author

A new way of life — homeschooling — began to evolve for me shortly after my children were born. Eagerly I watched my young learners joyfully discover their world. I began to question, and finally to discard, many of the notions I had held so closely about how children learn and grow.

Those traditional educational ideas had governed me while I taught in public and private schools for years. Now I found that many of those ideas interfered with the true and natural process of learning that I observed daily both with my children and with their friends. I began a one hundred eighty degree shift in my thinking, both about how children learn and about the purpose of schools.

I continued that turn-around in my thinking soon after I discovered John Holt's *Growing Without Schooling* newsletter in 1979. Relieved that I was not alone in my transition from teacher-centered schooling to interest-initiated learning, I began to "unschool" myself. I immersed myself in the thinking of John Holt and others who have explored the true nature of learning. I followed the stories and experiences of that first wave of pioneer homeschooling families.

With *GWS* as my "support group by mail," our family launched into homeschooling. We followed an eclectic, interest-driven curriculum. I quickly learned that my children's learning followed no calendar or clock. Both children were eager learners. Our lives were rich with the explorations and discoveries of two busy and happy children. They learned what they needed to know through experience, books, games, conversations, classes, and extensive play. They had ready access to their mom, and were supported by a dad who believed that there had to be a better way than school, and cheerfully provided the means.

Homeschooling with my children has provided me with the opportunity to continue my personal growth in ways that I had never considered. I have gone beyond schooling to find a true personal education, and my personal calling as a teacher and writer.

As a homeschooling parent, I found that I could offer my children and myself a precious opportunity to learn and grow that cannot be approached in other educational models.

I hope that this book helps other families to provide one-to-one help and encouragement in learning for all members of the family, to guide their children's learning even in difficult times, and to enjoy the experience along the way. Such an education cannot be purchased at any price. — *AL* —

❖ ❖ ❖

Index

M